Street by Street

CW00673399

CANNOCK, LI........
TAMWORTH
BROWNHILLS, BURNTWOOD, GREAT WYRLEY, HEDNESFORD, RUGELEY
Brereton, Cheslyn Hay, Fazeley, Hammerwich, Heath Hayes, Huntington, Norton Canes, Rawnsley, Wilnecote, Wimblebury

1st edition September 2002

© Automobile Association Developments Limited 2002

Ordnance Survey® This product includes map data licensed from Ordnance Survey® with the permission of the Controller of Her Majesty's Stationery Office. © Crown copyright 2002. All rights reserved. Licence No: 399221.

Published by AA Publishing (a trading name of Automobile Association Developments Limited, whose registered office is Millstream, Maidenhead Road, Windsor, Berkshire SL4 5GD. Registered number 1878835).

The Post Office is a registered trademark of Post Office Ltd. in the UK and other countries.

Schools address data provided by Education Direct.

One-way street data provided by:

Tele Atlas ◄ © Tele Atlas N.V.

Mapping produced by the Cartographic Department of The Automobile Association. A01100

A CIP Catalogue record for this book is available from the British Library.

Printed by GRAFIASA S.A., Porto, Portugal

The contents of this atlas are believed to be correct at the time of the latest revision. However, the publishers cannot be held responsible for loss occasioned to any person acting or refraining from action as a result of any material in this atlas, nor for any errors, omissions or changes in such material. This does not affect your statutory rights. The publishers would welcome information to correct any errors or omissions and to keep this atlas up to date. Please write to Publishing, The Automobile Association, Fanum House (FH17), Basing View, Basingstoke, Hampshire, RG21 4EA.

Ref: ML195

Key to map pages	ii-iii
Key to map symbols	iv-1
Enlarged scale pages	2-5
Street by Street	6-51
Index – towns & villages	52
Index – streets	53-62
Index – featured places	62-63

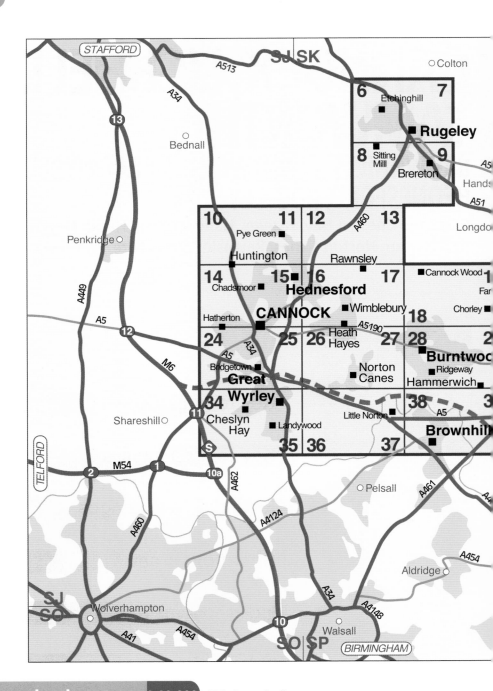

STAFFORD

A513

SJ SK

○ Colton

A34

6

Etchinghill ■

7

13

Bednall ○

Rugeley

8

Sitting
Milll ■

9

A5

Brereton ■

Hands

A51

10

11

12

A460

13

Longdo

Pye Green ■

Penkridge ○

Huntington

Rawnsley ■

14

15 ■

16

17

■ Cannock Wood

1

Chadsmoor ■

Hednesford

Far

A449

CANNOCK

■ Wimblebury

18

Chorley ■

A5

Hatherton ■

■

A5190

12

24

25

26

Heath
Hayes ■

27

28

2

M6

A5

A34

Norton
Canes ■

Burntwoo

Bridgetown ■

■ Ridgeway

Great

Hammerwich

38

3

Wyrley ■

34

A5

Shareshill ○

11

Cheslyn
Hay

Little Norton ■

Brownhil

S

■ Landywood

■

35

36

37

TELFORD

M54

2

1

10a

A462

○ Pelsall

A461

A4

A460

A4124

A454

SJ
SO

Aldridge ○

Wolverhampton ○

A34

A4148

10

○

Walsall

A41

A454

SO SP

kilometres

BIRMINGHAM

Enlarged scale pages   1:10,000   6.3 inches to 1 mile

0   1/4   miles   1/2

0   1/4   1/2   kilometres   3/4   1

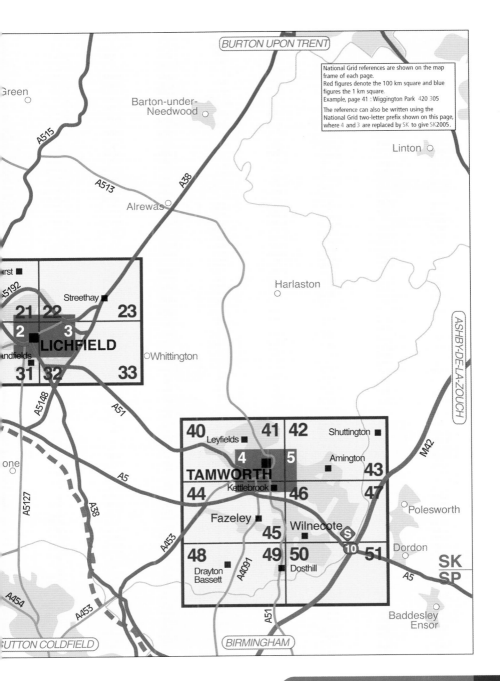

Green

BURTON UPON TRENT

National Grid references are shown on the map frame of each page.
Red figures denote the 100 km square and blue figures the 1 km square.
Example, page 41 : Wiggington Park 420 305

The reference can also be written using the National Grid two-letter prefix shown on this page, where 4 and 3 are replaced by SK to give SK2005.

Barton-under-Needwood

Linton

A515

A513

A38

Alrewas

Harlaston

ASHBY-DE-LA-ZOUCH

A5192

rst

Streethay

21 22 23

2 3

LICHFIELD

ndfields

Whittington

31 32 33

A5148

A51

40 Leyfields 41 42 Shuttington

one

A5 4 5 Amington

TAMWORTH 43

A5127

A38

44 Kettlebrook 46 47

Fazeley Wilnecote Polesworth

45 S Dordon

10 51

A454

A453 48 49 50 Dosthill

Drayton Bassett A4091 SK

A453 SP

A5

Baddesley Ensor

UTTON COLDFIELD

BIRMINGHAM

A51

M42

4.2 inches to 1 mile **Scale of main map pages 1:15,000**

0 1/4 miles 1/2 3/4 1

0 1/4 1/2 kilometres 3/4 1 1 1/4 1 1/2

Junction 9	Motorway & junction
Services	Motorway service area
	Primary road single/dual carriageway
Services	Primary road service area
	A road single/dual carriageway
	B road single/dual carriageway
	Other road single/dual carriageway
	Minor/private road, access may be restricted
← ←	One-way street
	Pedestrian area
============	Track or footpath
	Road under construction
⌐ - - - ⌐	Road tunnel
AA	AA Service Centre
P	Parking
P+🚌	Park & Ride
🚌	Bus/coach station
	Railway & main railway station
	Railway & minor railway station

⊖	Underground station
⊖	Light railway & station
+++++++++	Preserved private railway
LC	Level crossing
●—●—●—●	Tramway
------------	Ferry route
....	Airport runway
— · — · — · —	County, administrative boundary
ᚡᚡᚡᚡᚡᚡᚡ	Mounds
I7	Page continuation 1:15,000
3	Page continuation to enlarged scale 1:10,000
	River/canal, lake, pier
	Aqueduct, lock, weir
465 ▲ Winter Hill	Peak (with height in metres)
	Beach
	Woodland
	Park
	Cemetery
	Built-up area

	Featured building		Abbey, cathedral or priory
	City wall		Castle
A&E	Hospital with 24-hour A&E department		Historic house or building
PO	Post Office	Wakehurst Place NT	National Trust property
	Public library		Museum or art gallery
i	Tourist Information Centre		Roman antiquity
	Petrol station Major suppliers only		Ancient site, battlefield or monument
†	Church/chapel		Industrial interest
	Public toilets		Garden
	Toilet with disabled facilities		Arboretum
PH	Public house AA recommended		Farm or animal centre
	Restaurant AA inspected		Zoological or wildlife collection
	Theatre or performing arts centre		Bird collection
	Cinema		Nature reserve
	Golf course		Visitor or heritage centre
▲	Camping AA inspected		Country park
	Caravan Site AA inspected		Cave
	Camping & caravan site AA inspected		Windmill
	Theme park		Distillery, brewery or vineyard

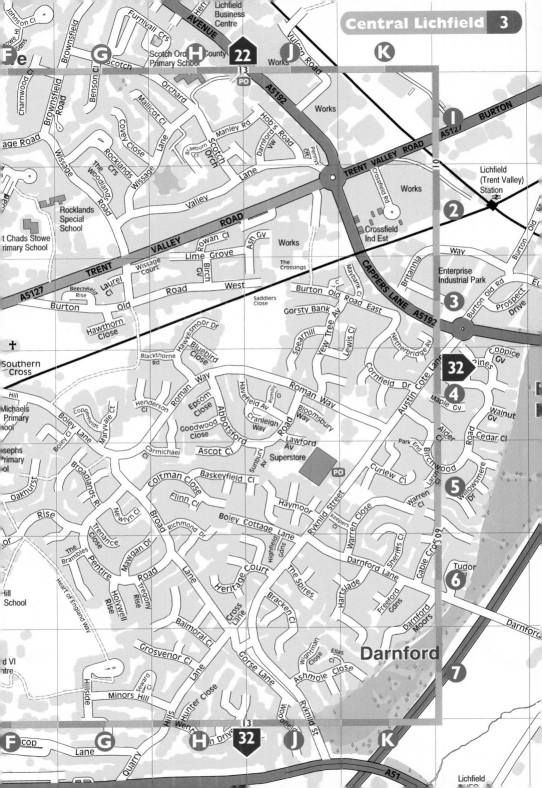

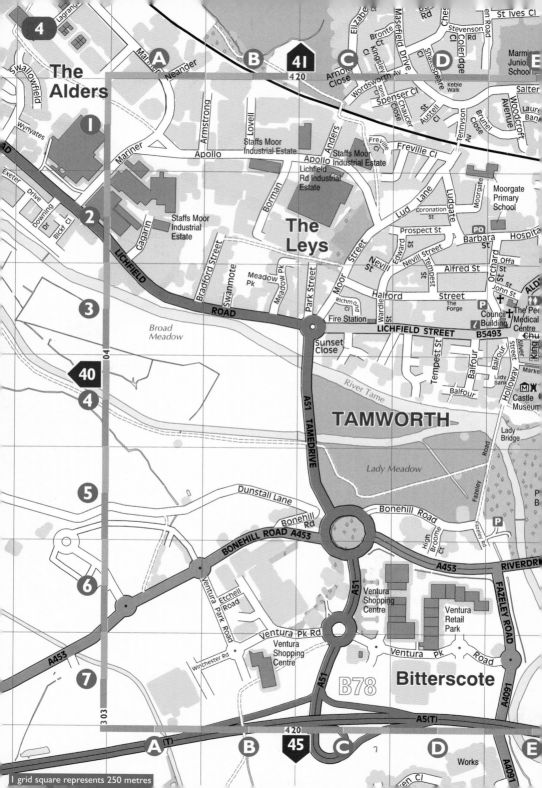

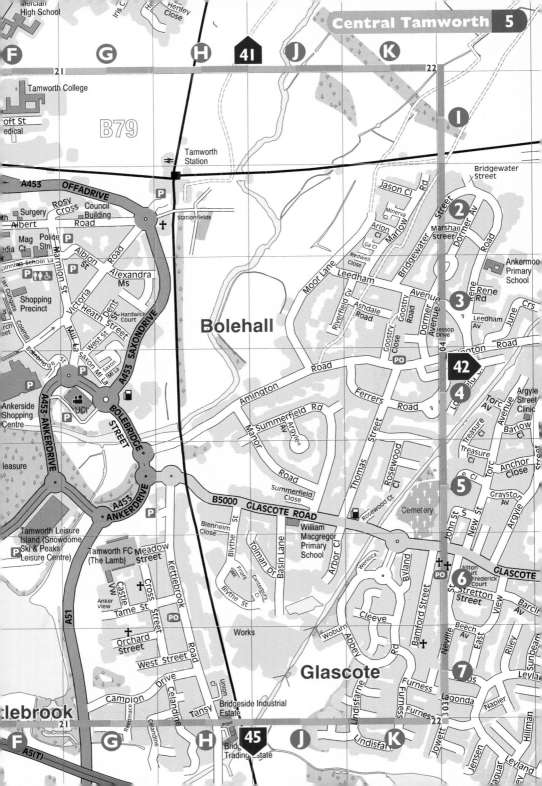

E F G H

WS15

Parchfield House

I

Blithb

2

Blithbury Road

Colton Hall Farm

B5013 COLTON ROAD

Rydal Estate

Trent Valley Trading Estate

Rugeley Trent Valley Station

3

B5013

Works

River Trent

WOLSELEY ROAD

Little Orch

Penwrth Av

Leyland Drive

Cern

Chancel Infant School

Boston Industrial Estate

Riverside

Stafford College

STATION ROAD

POWER

4

Trent Business Park

Power Stn Road Ind Estate

Red Rose Theatre

Taylor's Street

Phoenix Close

Tannery Close

Love Lane

Station Road

Aelfgar Sixth Form Centre

PO

Market St

ANSON ST

Bryans Lane

Leathermill Lane

Hotel

Bees Lane

Mill Lane

Forge Road

Brewery St

Heron Street

Queen St

King St

Cawa Farm

5

Albion

Lichfield St

ELMORE LANE

Upr Brook St

HORSE FAIR

Rugeley Health Centre

Wellington Dr

Talbot Street

Arch St

Lockside VW

Churchfield CE Junior School

SANDY LANE

A513

Wharf Road

LEY

Hill St

E

Rugeley Town Station

Pear Tree County Primary School

Hardle

Curzon Avenue

F

Attlee Crs

George Brealey

Newman Gv

9

Springfield Av

G

ARMITAGE

Trent View Close

Trent and Mersey Canal

Powe ... ion

H

8

The Stone
House

School

A B 6 C D Hag Sch

402 03 †

Quarry Cl

Oakley Copse

Jones Lane

Road Mill

Post Office Lane

Slitting Mill

I The Pingle

Millside Slitting

Birches Valley
Forest Centre

17

Slitting Mill River

Cardig Av

ROAD

Essex Drive Rt Av Durhac

2

Flaxley
Green

Surrey
Close

3

16

HEDNESFORD

4

Smart's
Buildings

A460

Stilecop
Field

Stile Cop Road

5

A460

LC

315

Moor's
Gorse

Lower
Cliff

'Regent's
Wood'

402 03

A B 13 C D

Marquis's Drive

1 grid square represents 500 metres

EY

HORSE FAIR

Rugeley Health Centre

Talbot Street

SAND LINE

Churchfield CE Junior School

E

Arch

F

Parkside Vw

7

05

G

06

H

Power Station

I

Rugeley Town Station

Wharf Road

Pear Tree County Primary School

Attlee Crs

Trent and Mersey Canal

ARMITAGE

ROAD

17

2

Newman Gv

Curzon Avenue

Hilltop

George Brealey Cl

Springfield Av

Trent View Close

St Josephs RC Primary School

The Laurels

Ravenhill Terrace

Garden Drive

Thorn Close

Works

BRERETON

Lichfield Swimming Pools & Spas

Canal View Business Park

Towers Business Park

Hardie

Ashleigh Road

Queensway

Springhill Ter

McKie Wy

Coulthwaite Way

Kelly Avenue

Beeches Rd

Oaktree Road

McCm Wy

The Grn

PO

A51

Sycamore Crs

Ashtree Bank

Lodge

Coalway Rd

Rg Ct

Arm Gdn

RUGELEY ROAD

The Shrubbery

Oakleigh Lane

The Meadow

Hislop Rd

Snaftsbury Rd

Hilliary Crest

Sutton Cl

Madden Cl

Corse Rise

Cm Vw Rd

The Grn

Ravenhill Prim Sch

Redbrook Close

Rowley Close

Walnut Ct

Lees Close

Thompson Rd

Hillside

Abbots Wk

Holly Bank View

County School

Heather

Corse Lane

Setterfield Way

Cherry Tree Rd

Talbot Road

St Michael's Road

St Mch Rd

Seabrooke Road

Hall

Abbots

Hobbs Vw

B MC

Stile Close

Birch

Redbrook Lane

Leasowe Road

Nursery Fields Prim Sch

Surgery

Lea Barn

Priory Road

Hobhill CE & Methodist Primary School

A513

Armitage Lane

3

Redbrook Lane Industrial Estate

Kimberley Way

The Levels

Nursery Rd

Cedar Crs

Swan Close

Lea

Armitage Lane

16

Chetwynd's Coppice

The Levels Industrial Estate

Brick Kiln Way

Redbrook Lane Industrial Estate

Coalpit Lane

Wattfield Cl

Twth Wlk

MAIN ROAD BRERETON

Batesway

A51

4

Colliery Road

Breretonhill

5

Brereton Lane

E

F

G

H

315

05

06

Brereton Hayes Wood

10

A · B · C · D

396 · 15 · 97 · Green

A34(T)

Broadhurst

Pottal
Valley

1 Keepers
Lodge

14

2 Yewtree
Farm

STAFFORD ROAD

3

Sycamore Wy
Silver
Birch
Rd
Almon
Maple Dr
Ash
Oak Tree Rd
Avenue
Cherry Gv
Elm Cl
Beech Gv
Lime Rd
Fir Cl
Rd
Hawthorne Rd
Hunts Rl
Wrekin Vw
Dual Wy
A34(T)
Huntington
CP School

4 Littleton
Business Park
Pear Tree Cl
Robin Cl
Holly La
Foxfields
Skylark
Redwing Dr
N Cl
STAFFORD ROAD
Linnet Cl
Littleton Dr
Woodstock
Dr
A Cl

5 Industrial
Estate
Gravel La
Mansty Farm
396
Oxin Cl
PO
Pillaton
Dr
Teddesley Wy
Stag Dr
Squirrel Cl
Badger
Hunting
Heathbank
Lichen Cl
STAFFORD ROAD

A · B · **14** · C · D

396 · 97 · Gra
Green
Bracken
Cl
Blueberry Cr
Heather Dr
Ling Rd
Corse
Fern Rd
Moss Cl
Rosemary
LOWH

1 grid square represents 500 metres

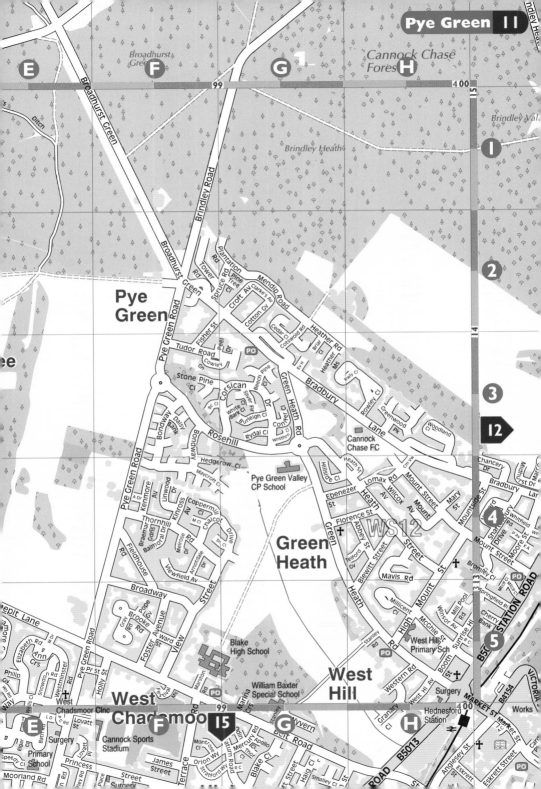

12

Marquis's Drive

A B C D

15 400 01

Brindley Valley

1

Cannock Chase
Country Park

2

West
Cannock Way

14

Slitting-Mill Rivera

A460

3

Bracken
Close

Walkers Rise

11

Crescent

Brindley

Heath Road

Chancer
Dr

Bradbury
Lane

Midhu

Marconi Pl

Edison Close

Bramble
Dr

1st Dr

Mountside St

Howard
Cl

Whitfield

Moors

PAVE St
Ws Pl

Lobden Cl

BD

RUGELEY

ROAD

4

Mount Street Av

Mount
St

Mary
St

Shaftesbury
Drive

Mount Street

Sandpiper Cl

Green
Industrial
Estate

Green
Slade
Gv

Sunley
Hill

Stringers
Hill

Denmark
Rise

Bromley Cl

Rd Rd

Springfield Rd

Mill Pool Cl

313

Cherry
Bank

PO

Beverley
Hill

Glendene
Road

Heather Valley

Valley Road

The Museum of
Cannock Chase

M

Rawnsley Road

5

West Hill
Primary Sch

Mount

Winsor Av

McChie

Booth St

West Hl
Av

High

STATION ROAD

B5013

MAP 400

A460

VICTORIA STREET

Surgery

Hednesford
Station

B4154

Works

Market St

Caradian
Place

HEDNESFORD

A B C D

16 01

**Church
Hill**

B5013

Long esley St

Street

PO

1 grid square represents 500 metres

A460

E

Moor's Gorse

F

Low Cliff

8
03

G

Regent's Wood

H

04
15

Marquis's Drive

I

Wandon

2

Upper Cliff

14

3

Beau Desert Golf Club

Sukers Lodge

4

Heart of England Way

5

Golf Course

313

PO

Rugeley Road

Hazel Slade Primary School

Hazelslade

Cannock Wood

Cannock Wood Industrial Estate

04

Holly

Beanbeam

Alder Wy

Cypress Valley Road

Fernfield

Painfield Wy

Jnw Rd

Eastgate

St Patrick

St David Dr

Old Pk Rd.

St Matthew Cl

George

St Thomas Close

St Andrew

Snaw Cl K C

BB BLU

SSFC

Rawnsley
03

17

F

G

H

Chapel Lane

Littleworth Road

Surgery

Chetwynd Park

Cann

New

W

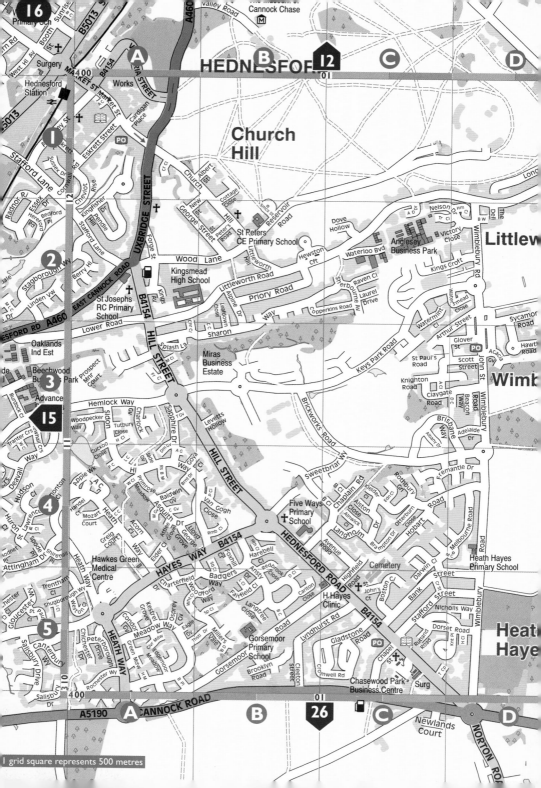

E **F** **13** **G** **H**

03 04

Rawnsley

Cannock Wood Industrial Estate

Eastgate
St Patrick
St Thomas
St Andrew
George David
Dr
Matthew
Dr
St FC
B B La
Old Pk Rd

Littleworth Road

Surgery

Chetwynd
Park

Cannock & Rugeley
Cricket Club

New
Hayes

I

Holly
Chapel Lane
Cur

12

Cannock Wood Road

New Hayes Road

2

Williamson Av
Longstaff Av
St Bernards Close
Danby Dr
Briars Wy

**Prospect
Village**

Ironstone

Ironstone Road

3

Sevens Road

Ironstone Road

18

4

Kingsdown Roa

Littleton
Way

Mayor Av

Lea Hall
Drive

5

Holly
Grove
Primary
School
Angel
Cft

Holly Grove Lane
Mowbray

03 04

E **F** **27** **G** **H**

The Grovey
Fair

Bleak House Dr
The
Valley

Drive

Gullick Way

School Lane

Ironstone Road

**Cha
Terr**

PO

Park Cft
Hilton
Wembley Lane

Radmore
School Cft
Thorpe Street
School Wk
Chapel

School

18

404

05

A B C D

Cannock Wood

Darling's Hayes

Heart of England Way

Malt House Rd

Ring

Hill
Baden Powell Close
Cilwell Road
Pineside Avenue
High Meadow
The Firs
Chestall Road

Holly
Chapel Lane
Park Gate
Road
Bradwell La
Sycamore Hl
U Cl

Cumberledge
Hill
Slang Lane
Ivy Lane
Buds Road

School Lane
Common Side
Gentleshaw Primary School

Windmill Bank
Cok
We

1

12

2

Chapel Lane
Gentleshaw
Briertey

Hayfield Hill

Hayfield Hill

Windmill Lane
Shaw Lane
Bre

Redmoor Road

3

17

Common Side

4

Chorley Road

Duke Rd
Viscount
Knowl Rd
Chorley Road
Squirrels Hollow
Boney Hay Primary School
Heath View
Ogley
Hay Road
Meg Lane

Kingsdown Road
Earl Drive
Baron Cl
Lance Dr
The Crs
Chrly Rd
Bells Lane
Byron Rd
low Rd
Beaudesert
Boney Hay

5
Mayor Av
Littlet Way
Lea Hall Drive
Holly Grove Primary School
Angel Cft
Railway Lane
Hill Lane
Melford Rd
Lymington Rd
MntB Cl
Chrly Rd
North St
May Close
Wesley Close
Longfel
Surgery
Oak Lane
Birch Terrace
Chaucer
Shelley Rd
Tiny Rd
A C

Bleak House Dr
Lady Drive
School Lane
Ironstone
Redmore Rd
School Wk
Cft Cl
St
High Street
Rugeley Road
Spinney
Chasewater Heaths Business Park
M Cl

404

05

A
Chase Terrace
Estgate
Spencer Drive
Cross Street
Park Road
Shakespeare Road
Californian Gv
Rbnsn Rd
Lebano

B
Coppice Close
Beechen Grove
Alden Hurst
Redwood Drive

28
Ryecroft Shopping Centre
Aspen
Linden Av

C
Fernleigh
Parkhill Rd
Blenheim Road
Slade Avenue
Ti
Deal
Osworth Rd
Ryecroft Rd
Brackenhill
Croft Gdns
Wilkinson Close

D R
Sanderling Rise
Brunel Close
Hunsl

PO

I grid square represents 500 metres

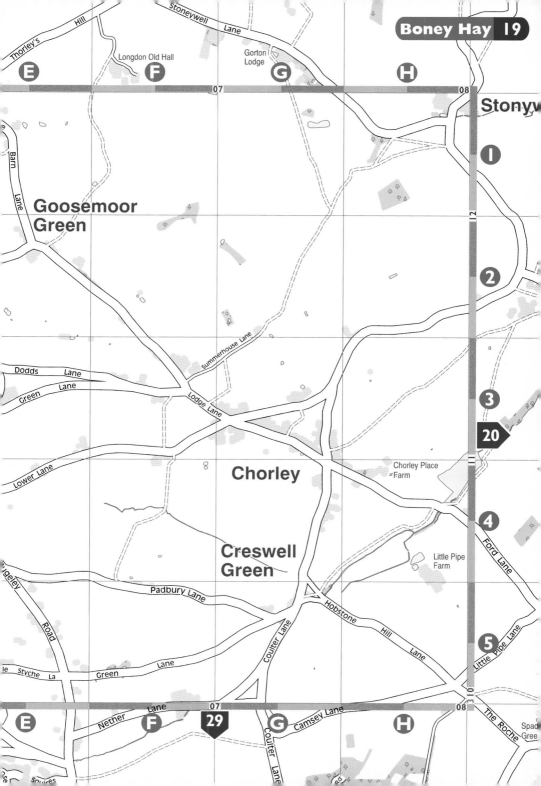

Thorley's Hill

Stoneywell Lane

Longdon Old Hall

Gorton Lodge

E   **F**   **G**   **H**

07   08

Stonyw

1

12

Barn Lane

Goosemoor Green

2

Summerhouse Lane

Dodds Lane

Green Lane

Lodge Lane

3

20

Lower Lane

Chorley

Chorley Place Farm

4

Creswell Green

Little Pipe Farm

Ford Lane

ngeley Road

Padbury Lane

Coulter Lane

Hobstone Hill Lane

Little Pipe Lane

5

styche La

Green Lane

E   **F**   **29**   **G**   Camsey Lane   **H**

Nether Lane

07   08

Coulter Lane

The Roche

Spa

Gree

Squires

Hall Farm

Nash Lane

Elmhurst

Fox Lane

TEWNALS

A515

Binns Farm

Lea Grange

Grange Lane

BED LANE

EASTERN AVENUE A5192

Watery Lane

Worcester Cl

Truro Close

St Mary's Rd

St Ctr

Curborough Road

Field Rd

Barn Close

Fallow

Meadowbrook

Ringwo Indust Estate

Tra

22

Lincoln Close

Charnwo County Primary S

Friary Grange Sports Centre

Giles Road

St Margarets Road

Harwood Rd

Simpson Road

Sheph Close

ROAD A51

The Friary School

EASTERN AVENUE A5192

Francis Road

Dimbles

Bimfl

Willows Primary School

Purcell

Avenue

Purcell Avenue

Walkers Croft

Nethertowe

Wolsey Road

Carrick Road

Newton Road

Oakenfield

Collins Hill

Lane

Langton Medical Group

Elgar Close

Ponesgreen

Stychbrook Gardens

Poneshield Road

Stowe

Pipers Croft

Greencroft

Booth Close

The Garth

WESTERN BY-PASS

Cross In Hand La

Stafford Road

Ferndale

Grange Lane

High

Longstaff Croft

Windmill Lane Close

Weston

Leyfields

Nether Stowe County High School

Lyn Avenue

Orchard Close

Ferndale Road

Martin Croft

Giffords Croft

Friday Acre

Chadsmead Primary School

Crane Field

Wood Ridings

Dimbles Hill

Audnleck

Beacon Street

Lynfield Road

Hayes Wk

Abnalls Lane

Patrick Mews

Wheel Lane

Swallow Croft

The Leasowe

St Peter & St Paul RC Primary School

PO

St Chad's Road

5

Cemetery

Lane

31

Work

PO

Beacon Street

Swinfen

Brown

Beacon Street

Gala Lane

Little Barrow Walk

Nether Beacon

Woods Croft

Lomax Rd

Anson Avenue

Prince Ruperts Way

The Windings

Lichfield C ral School (Bishops Palace)

Erasmus Darwin Centre

Lichfield Cath

Cross Keys

Stowe Pool

Stowe Rd

Drake Croft Mallard Rd Smithfield

Partridge Croft

George

Frank

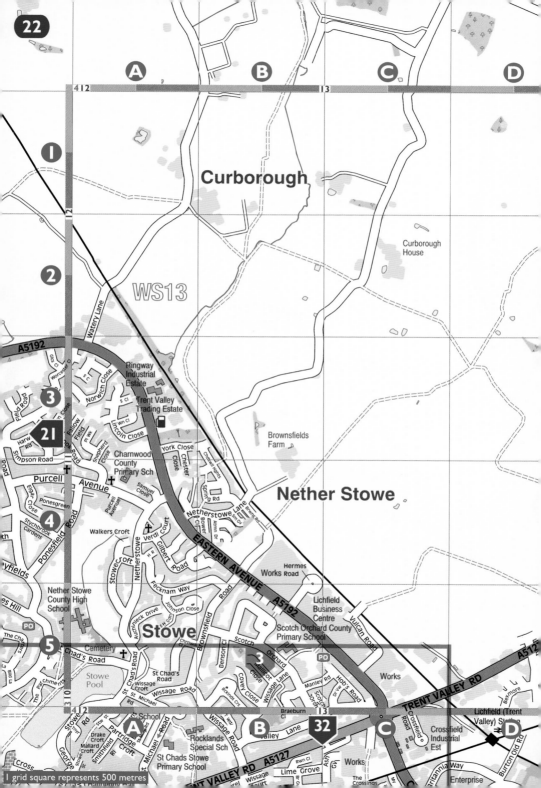

22

A B C D

412 13

1

Curborough

2

Curborough House

WS13

A5192

Ringway Industrial Estate

Trent Valley Trading Estate

3

21

Charnwood County Primary Sch

Brownsfields Farm

York Close
Chester Close
Creswell Heights

Spring Rd

Nether Stowe

Purcell Avenue

Ponesgreen
Elms Close

4

Walkers Croft

Verdi Court

Gilbert Road

Netherstowe

Stowecroft

Fecknam Way

Johnson Close

Hermes Works Road

Lichfield Business Centre

Scotch Orchard County Primary School

Nether Stowe County High School

Auchinleck Drive

Vulcan Road

Stowe

Brownsfield Road

3

Benson Rd

scotch

Orchard Road

Hob's Road

Works

5

St Chad's Road

Cemetery

St Chad's Road

Stowe Pool

Wissage Road

Covey Close
Talllis Cl

Wissage Lane

Manley Rd

PO

TRENT VALLEY RD

A51

Lichfield (Trent Valley) Station

310

412 13

Crossfield Industrial Est

Crossfield Road

A **B** **32** **C** **D**

School

Drake Croft
Mallard Croft
Smithfield

Partridge Croft

Rocklands Special Sch

St Chads Stowe Primary School

Braeburn Cl

Valley Lane

Works

Burton Old Rd

Britannia Way

Enterprise

TRENT VALLEY RD A5127

Lime Grove

The Crossings

1 grid square represents 500 metres

Worthington

Forrest

Coventry Canal

A38(T)

E

F

G

H

I

Industrial
Estate

5

6

Common Lane

Blenheim   Way

Lancaster Rd

Ironstone

LC

**Hilliard's
Cross**

East
Hill

Business
Park

Wood End Lane

Brookhay Lane

LC

2

Wellington Crescent

Wood End Lane

Bears Hay
Farm

Mare Brook

Brookhay

3

Thatchmoor
Farm

Streethay

A38(T)

4

A38(T)

Broad Lane

Whitting
Farm

Hill
Farm

5

310

E

F

33

G

H

15

16

Broad Lane

Park   Lane

Park

E F 17 G H

Mavor Av

Holly Grove Primary School
Holly Grove Lane
Angel Cft

The Grovev Fair Lady Drive
Bleak House Dr
The Valley
Gullick Way
Radmore
Wembley Lane
Park Cft
Fives Hilton GV
Two Oaks Av
School Lane
School Wk
School Close
Thorpe Street
Chapel Street
PO
Ironstone Road
Chas Terr
I
Lorne Street
Princess St

CANNOCK ROAD A5190

Thorpe Av
Thorpe Close

Griffin Close

Chaselands

Chasewater Heaths Business Park

Attwood Road
Cobbett Road

Chase Park Industrial Estate

Plant Lane

No Name Rd

2

Norton Canes School

Deer Close
Grange Road
Burntwood Road
Lakeside Dr

Ring Road
Cannel Rd
Cinder Road
Smith's Close
Robins

Benches Close

3

Stag Crs
School Road
School Close
School Crs

Norton East

Norton Canes Primary School

Poplar Street

PO
Railway Street

Norton East Road

Pool Av
St James Rd

Park Rd
Park Av

Breeze Avenue
PO

28

Church

4

Elunda
308

Tree Road

Brownhills Road
Newbury Rd

High Street

Elm Road
Cherry Tree Road
Silver Birch Road
Brownhills Road

Chasewater

Chase High Sc

5

duit Road
strial Est
duit
Knights Court
Lane
n Canes
ess Park

Red Lion Crs
Red Lion Av
Blenheim Road
Braemar Road
Red Lion Lane

Chasewater Light Railway

E F 37 G H

Proposed Service Area

Chase Watersports Centre

Albutts Road

E F **19** G H

Coulter Lane

Stuche La

Road

Green Lane

Nether Lane

Camsey Lane

Coulter Lane

Little P...

Hi... Lane

The Roche

Spa... Gre

I

Cavell Rd

Freer Dr

Gregory Rd

Nightingale Wk

Sister Dora Av

St Matthew's Avenue

St Matthew's

St

Close

Squires Gate

N C

Trevithick Close

Wentworth Close

Highfields Primary School

Laurel Dr

Browning Rd

Lea

Fulfen

Fulfen Primary School

Gorstey

Gorsley Ley

Chaseley Gdns

Rose La

Bracken Cl

Burns Drive

Poole's Way

Church Road

Scholars Gate

Hamps Cl

Penk Cl

Tean Close

Leam Drive

Stour Cl

Canterbury Drive

Cemetery

Glasscroft Cottages

Jones' Lane

Woodhouses Lane

Woodhouses Road

Wood

2

A5190

Swanfields

PO

Shopping Swan Corner Centre

Burntwood Health Centre

St Paul's Rd

St Mark's Road

Fairford Gdns

Huson Dr

Dewsbury Drive

Blandford Gdns

Nailers Drive

Mease Av

Severn Dr

Derwent Gv

Dove Cl

Tame Av

Anker Cl

Trent Close

Blythe

Farewell Lane

Burntwood Green

Forge Lane

3

Willow Av

Lime Grove

Maidstone

Meadow View

Norton Lane

Hammerwich Road

Norton Lane

LICHFIELD ROAD A5190

Edial

30

...ters

4

Stockhay Lane

Oaklands Academy of Theatre Dance

Nook Lane

Siskin Cl

Redwing Close

Forge Cl

Fieldfare

Pingle Lane

Burntwood Road

5

Overton Lane

Mansion Dr

Blackroot Close

Hammerwich

PO

Av

Mill Lane

Ch

Hall Lane

Meerash Lane

E F **39** G H

...nerwich

Coppice

grid square represents 500 metres

E   F   **23**   G   H

15

16

I Park

10

Hill Farm

Broad Lane

Park Lane

Huddlesford

2

Capper's Lane

Huddlesford Lane

09

Whittington Grange Special School

Swan Road

Burton Road

3

Neal Cft

Pass Av

Capper's Lane

Lane

Blacksmith La

Langton Cfs

Back Bramley Wy

Chapel Lane

Main St.

Darnford Lane

Ellfield House

Church Street

Babbington Cl

4

Marsh Lane

Beechwood

Windmill Hill

Whittington Common Road

08

Whittington Primary School

Sandy Lane

5

Golf Course

15

16

E   F   G   H

Worcester Rd

Heath Avenue

Stafford Crescent

Common Lane

Whittington Heath Golf Club

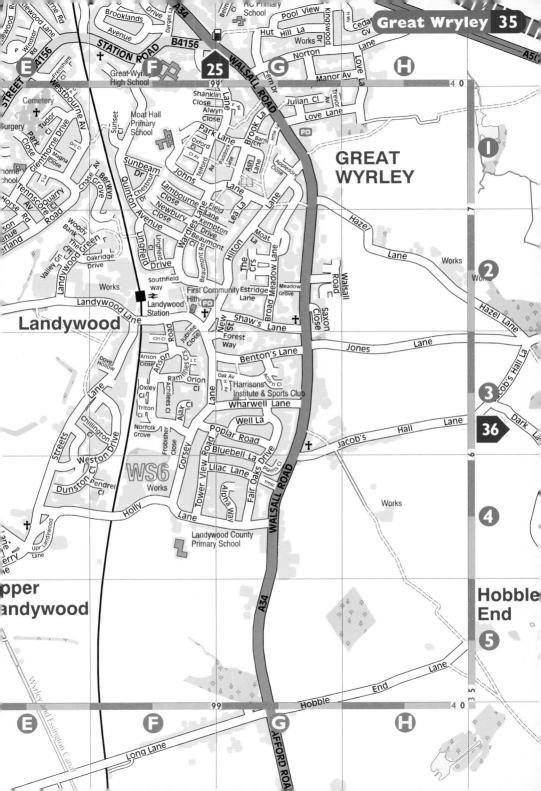

A5(
A34

E
wood Lane
Brooklands
Drive
Darges La A34
Belm
RC Primary
School
Pool View
Cedar
CV
Kingswood
Dr
H
Windsor
Rd
Frensham
Cl
STATION ROAD
B4156
Hut Hill La
Works
Norton

4156
Westbourne Av
Great Wryley
High School
25
WALSALL ROAD
Love La
Manor Av
F
Fern Dr
G
Love La
H

Cemetery
Surgery
Tudor
Cl
Park
Close
Glenthorne Drive
Magna
Close
Shanklin
Close
Alwyn
Close
Park Lane
Brook La
Julian Cl
Trevor
Cl
PO
Love Lane
I

horne
School
Tenniscore Av
Quarry
Rd
Chase Av
Berwin Grove
Sunset
Cl
Moat Hall
Primary
School
Oxford
Cl
Ct Av
Telford
Av
Ash La
Appledore
GREAT
WYRLEY

Horse Rd
Woody
Bank
The Green
Oakridge
Drive
Sunbeam
Dr
Quinton Avenue
Chestnut
Johns
Lane
Lambourne Cl
Newbury
Close
Field
Lane
Kempton
Drive
Beaumont
Lea La
Hilton
Moat
La
Haze
Lane
Works

Valley Gn
Landywood
Cr
Lingfield
Drive
Lingfield
Works
Ward
Cl
The
Crs
Southfield
Way
Landywood
Station
Estridge
Lane
Broad Meadow Lane
Meadow
Grove
Walsall
Road

Landywood
Landywood Lane
First Community
Hlth
PO
New
Shaw's Lane
Saxon
Close
Works

Dove
Hollow
Cin Cl
Jubilee Crs
Anson
Road
Anson
Close
Forest
Way
Benton's Lane
Jones Lane
Jacob's Hall La

Streets
Lane
Chillington Drive
Ramillies Crs
Achilles Cl
Orion
Cl
Oxley
Cl
Triton
Cl
Ajax Cl
Oak Av
Harrisons'
Institute & Sports Club
Wharwell Lane
Hall Lane
Dark La
36

Weston Cl
Dunston Cl
Pendrel
Cl
Norfolk
Grove
Frobisher Close
Corsey
Tower View Road
Poplar Road
Bluebell La
Well La
Jacob's
Hall La
Plant's La
Works

WS6
Works
Holly
Lane
Lilac Lane
Fair Oaks Drive
Alpha Way

Upr Landywood
Lane
Landywood County
Primary School
Hobble
End

pper
andywood

Wyrley and Essington Canal
A34
WALSALL ROAD
AFFORD ROAD
Hobble
End
Lane

E
F
G
Hobble
H

Long Lane

I
2
3
4
5

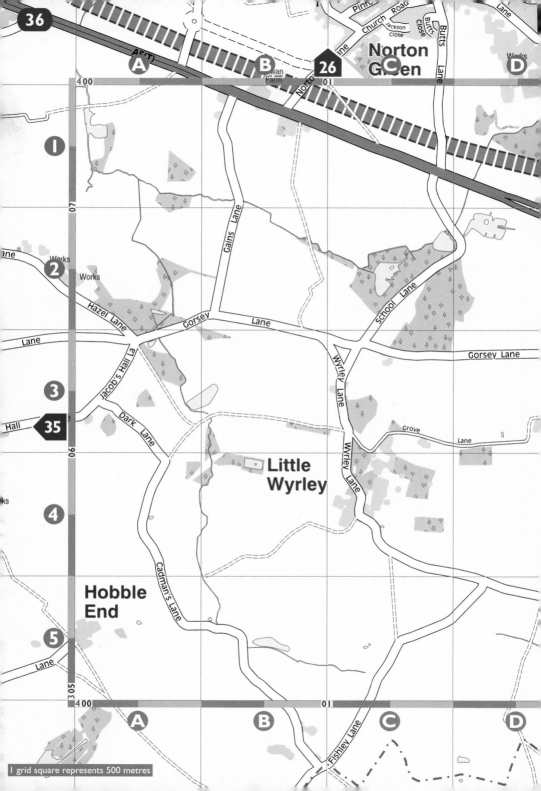

36

A(T)

A

B

26

Pinf...

Church Road

Jackson Close

Butts Close

Norton Line

Lane

Norton Green

C

Butts Lane

Works

D

400

01

Swan Farm

I

07

Lane

Works

2

Works

Hazel Lane

Gains Lane

Gorsey

Lane

School Lane

Lane

Gorsey Lane

Lane

Jacob's Hall La

Wyrley Lane

3

Hall

35

Dark Lane

Grove

Lane

4

Little Wyrley

Wyrley Lane

06

Hobble End

Cadman's Lane

5

305

Lane

400

01

A

B

Fishley Lane

C

D

I grid square represents 500 metres

Chasewater

Chase Watersports Centre

M6 Toll due to open Jan 2004

Chasewater Light Railway

Albutts Road

Proposed Service Area

Beacon Way

Hednesford Road

Poole Crescent

Beacon Way

Pool Road

PO

Lawnoaks Cl

Shewood Close

Watling Street Business Park

A5(T)

Little Norton

Maxfields Drive

Blithfield Road

Cherwell Drive

Pear Tree Lane

Cherwell Drive

Tyne Cl

Tamar Cl

Kennet Close

Shannon

Severn Road

Medway Rd

Wilkin Road

Waterside Way

Drive

Brownhills West JMI School

Watling Str JMI School

A452 CHESTER ROAD

Chester Rd

Bradford Road

Birch Av

Wallace Road

Hussey Road

Albion Road

Wyrley Common

Beacon Way

Coppice Lane

Engine Lane

West Coppice Road

Coppice Side

Coppice Side Industrial Estate

Croft Crescent

Coppice Crescent

Northfields Way

Staffordshire County Walsall

Collier Close

Apex Road

PELSALL ROAD

Pelsall Road

Clifton Av

Honest

Close

Larksp

Bell Heather Rd

Rosemary

Way

Holly

Emerdale Cl

Branstale Rd

Dunnerdale Road

Alferdale Road

Rushbrook

Clayhanger Lane

Beacon Way

A4124

Bullows Road

Cornflower Road

Crowberry Close

Snapdr

Holy Trinity

Bridge

E F 27 G H

I

2

3

4

5

E F G H

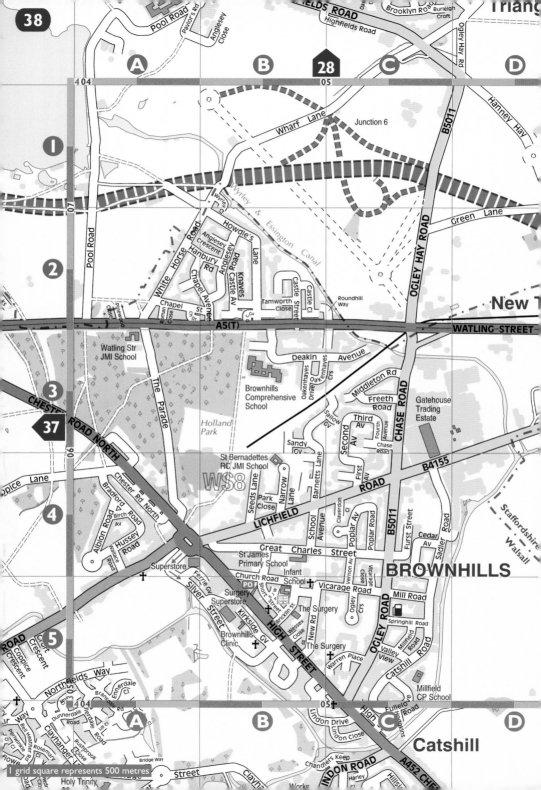

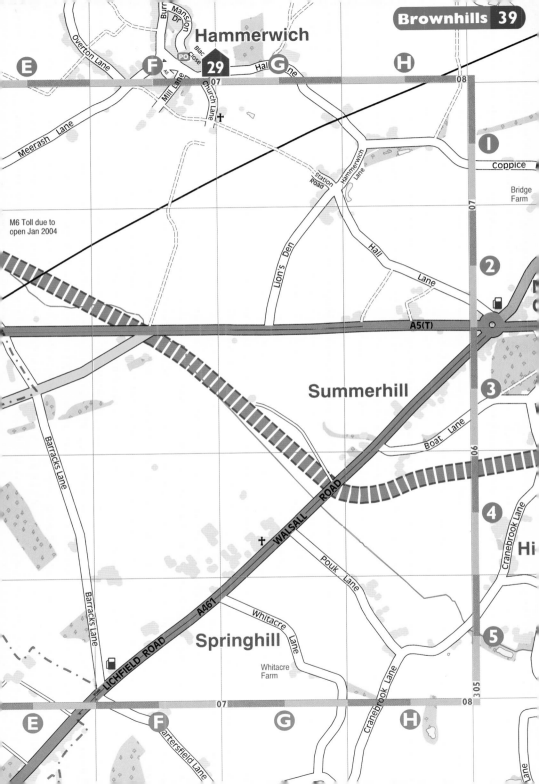

Hammerwich

Burr
Manson Dr
Blac Close
PO
Overton Lane
Hal ne
29
07
08

E
F
G
H

Mill Lane
Church Lane
†

Meerash Lane

Hammerwich Lane

Coppice

I

07

Bridge Farm

Station Road

M6 Toll due to
open Jan 2004

Lion's Den

Hall Lane

2

A5(T)

Summerhill

3

Boat Lane

06

Barracks Lane

4

Cranebrook Lane

Hi

WALSALL ROAD

†

Pouk Lane

Barracks Lane

A461

Whitacre Lane

Whitacre Farm

5

LICHFIELD ROAD

Springhill

Cranebrook Lane

07
3 05
08

E
F
G
H

Fartersfield Lane

A   B   C   D

06   418   19

1

Thomas Hays Wood

The Woodhouse

Coton Hall Farm

2

Thomas Barnes CP School

Coton Lane

Helmingham

Kentwell   Chartwell

Lorton

Longleat

Mariner   Kepler

Ariane

Lichfield Crescent

School Lane

Daintry Dr

LICHFIELD ROAD A51

Godolphin

Gwyab

Littict

Road

Gerard

Cavon

Lichfield Road Industrial Est

Hopwas

Church Drive

PO

Buckingham

Browsholme

Melford

Newstead

Lichfield Trading Est

HOPWAS HILL

Nursery Lane

Braham

Coton

Rufford

Thoresby

Swallowfield Wy

3

05

Hints Lane

Lane

Tr Dr

Oxbridge

Mnhd

LICHFIELD

Lane

Dunstall Lane

Gryl Dr

Way

Exeter Dr

Hints

4

Downing

304

Hints Lane

PLANTATION

Dunstall Farm

5

The Bodnets

LANE

Birmingham & Fazeley Canal

Dunstall Lane

LANE   418   19

A   B   **44**   C   D

B5404

Bonehill

1 grid square represents 500 metres

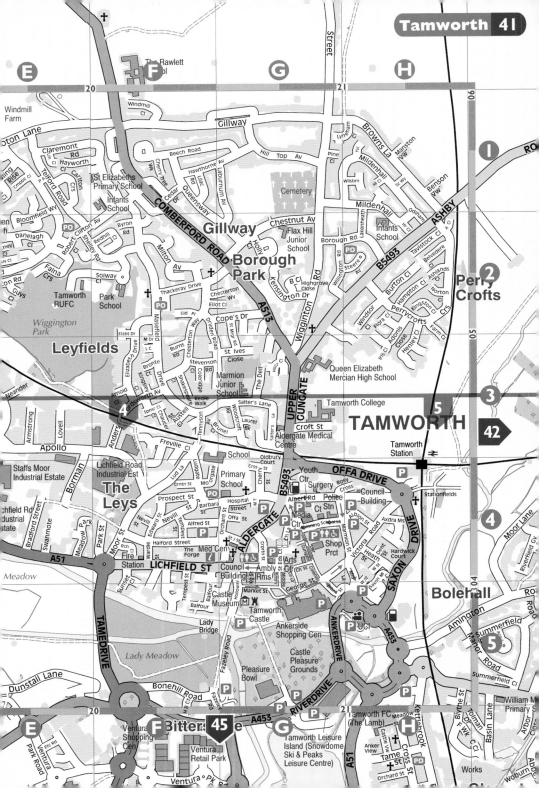

Grid references (top): 42, A, B, C, D, 4 22, 23

Left side grid numbers: I, 2, 3, 41, 4, 5

Bottom grid references: A, B, 46, C, D, 4 22, 23, B50

Place and street names:

Ashlands Farm

River Anker

Amington Hall

Amington Hall Farm

ASHBY ROAD

Swanston

Benson Wy

Tavistock Cl

Belvedere

Odiham Cl

Perry Crofts

Hampton Cl

Norton Cl

Kingston Crs

Crofts Farm

Henley Cl

Moor Farm

Moor Lane

Tom Hartley Park Homes

Bracklesham Wy

Caister

...worth Station

Stationfields

DRIVE

Jason Cl

Marlow Road

Ridgewater Street

Dormer Av

Rene Road

Leedham Av

Moor Lane

Riverfield Gv

Ashdale Rd

Goostry Rd

Jessop Drive

Lune Crs

Ld Av

Mrshll

Mnr Cl

Primary School

Whitesands

Whitley Av

Selker Av

Stonehaven

Emberton Wy

PO

Durston

Falmouth Dr

Brancaster

Woodhouse

Surgery

Ridgewood

Sharpe Street

Talland Avenue

Waterside Court

Tamworth Road

(Amington)

Florendine Primary School

Florendine St

Fairview

Ingram Pit La

Harebell

Bolehall

Amington Road

Summerfield Rd

Ferrers Road

Thomas Street

Rosewood Cl

Manor Road

Summerfield Cl

Longford Cl

Argyle Street Clnc

Torc Av

Barlow St

Warwick Rd

Treasure

Castle Av

Grayston Av

Anchor St

New St

Frederick St

St George's Way

Wesley St

St Mary's St

Lavender Rd

Rosemary Rd

Hanbury Rd

Davis Rd

Beechwood Crs

Sheepcote Lane

Tudor Crs

Tudor Dr

Oaklands Dr

Amington

Greenheart

Foxglove

Cornel

Woodland Rd

Jasmine

Hornbeam

Juniper

William Macgregor Primary School

Cemetery

Canning Road

Woodlands Primary School

Lichfield Road Industrial Estate

Angelica

Clematis

Brookweed

Briar

Kettlebrook

Basin Lane

Blythe St

Tolman

F Wk

C Cl

Bamford St

Cleeve

Neville St

Stretton St

Barcliff Av

Beech Vw

Camden Cl

Dumolo's

PO

Abelia

GLASCOTE ROAD

Glascote

grid square represents 500 metres

Tamworth Municipal Golf Club

Golf Course

43

Warwickshire County

Staffordshire County

E F G H

24 Dr

St Andrews Way

Troon

Eagle Cl

Merclan

Pebble Cl

Tamworth Bus Park

Amber Cl

Tamworth Business Centre

Silica Rd

cil ng

Galena Cl

Sandy Wy

Mica Cl

Lodge Farm

Amington Industrial Estate

Robey's Lane

Works

I

03

2

Pooley Lane

Calder

B5000 GLASCOTE ROAD

Ealingham

Ealingham

Edale

Edale

Blackdown

Amcm

Cleasby

Crr

Cheviot

Crgd

Crmal

Chiltern

Deerhill

Drstn

Dpdl

Rd

Dpdr

Bellingham

Broadlee

Tamworth Rd

TAMWORTH ROAD

Tamworth Road

The

Lyn

Ellerbeck

Health Centre

PO

Ellerbeck

Stoneydelph

Brendon

Beck

Loughshaw

Lowdham

Mendip Wy

Broadlee

Broadlee

3

Kiln Wy

Ensor

Lintly

Lintly

Litton

Malham

Lowforce

Maldale

Road

Marrick

Mll

Melmerby

Hermitage

Dark La

Lane

Spinney Cl

Woodland Wy

Dex

Fo

PENNINE

Lothersdale

Lothersdale

Mrtn

MVburn

Middlesmoor

Green Lane

4

Ae Cl

Road

ebden

WAY

Malham Road

Mornley

MsSd

Mickleton

Mayfield

Marsett

Rd

Poleswo High Sc

Raygill

Pennymoor Rd

Rrbkld

Rainscar

Rvnstn

Birchmoor Road

5

New St

Green Lane

Cockspur Street

Birchwood Primary Sch

Birch Gv

Birchmoor

Sykm

Tanhill

NW

T P R

WS

Torside

A5(T)

Green La

Hotel

La

Relay Dr

Green La

Green

Tamworth Service Area

24 25

E F G H

M

51

King Cr

Works

Junction 10

Dordo

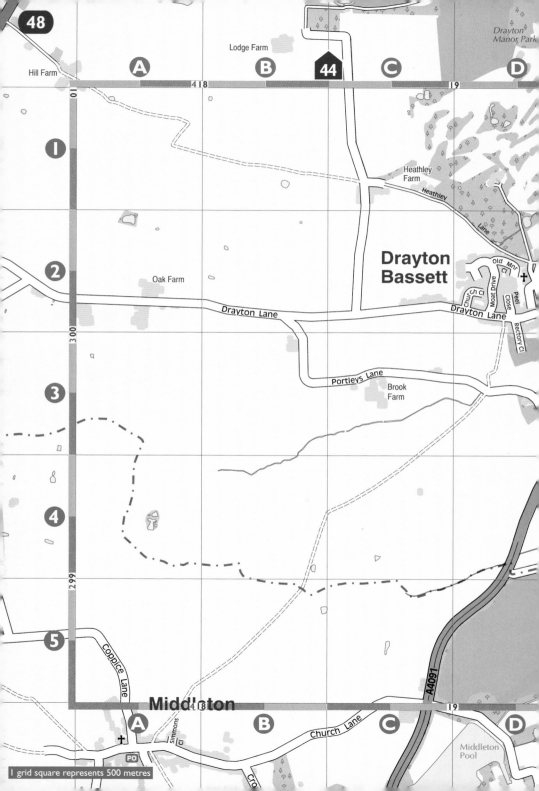

48

Hill Farm

Lodge Farm

44

Drayton Manor Park

Heathley Farm

Heathley Lane

Drayton Bassett

Old Mnr Cl

Church Cl

Moat Drive

Peel Close

Rectory Cl

Oak Farm

Drayton Lane

Drayton Lane

Portleys Lane

Brook Farm

Coppice Lane

5

Middleton

Simmons Cl

Church Lane

A4091

Middleton Pool

PO

Cro

I grid square represents 500 metres

COLESHILL RD

drayton Manor Drive

E   **F**   45   **G**   **H**

DOSTHILL RD

A51

20   21

Chill

Arundel
Road

Belvo

Whiting

Dace

Dorado

Grayling

Dosthill
House

I

Cottage Farm

Marlin

Kurtus   Lamprey

Kurtus   Manta

Kurtus

Dl H L2

A4091

Heart of England Way

River Tame

Dosthill

Orchard Cl

Greenhill
Cl

Welford
Rd

Welford Rd

Park Rd

Skidmore Av

Tolson Cl

TAMWORTH ROAD (DOSTHILL)

B4300

School

2

Surg

Cadogan

La

Par

Dosthill School

Arkle

Arkle

Larksp

Nim

Mrst

Church
Rd

Maxstoke Cl

Slade Lane

HIGH ST

Roseberry Road

Se

3

Lochso
Ci

A51

Felstead
Cl

Hatwo

Epsom Cl

Asco

50

ws Brook

Heart of England Way

4

Rush Lane

B299

A51

5

TAMWORTH

ROAD

Heart of

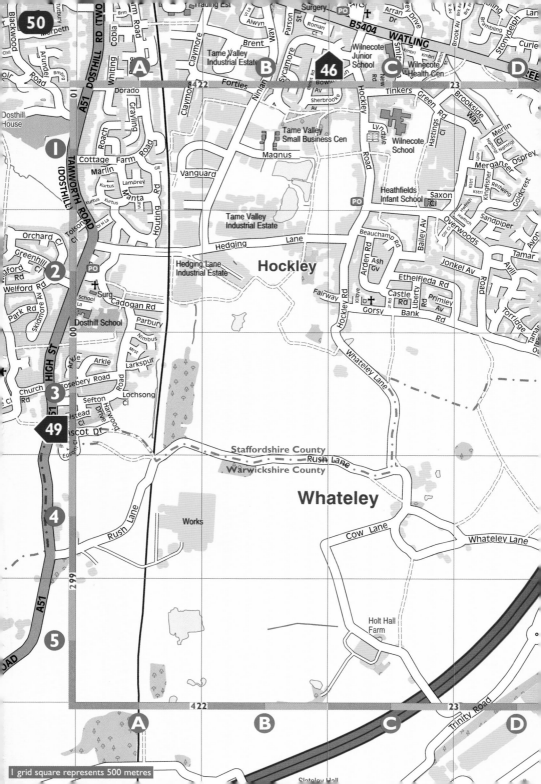

I grid square represents 500 metres

Birchmoor

E
(T)
24

F Tamworth Service A

Hotel
La

Relay Dr

47

G

25
01

H

I

Dordo

Works

Kinsal

Green La

M42

Junction 10

Centurion Way

WATLING

STREET

Hall E

Birch Coppice
Industrial Estate

Birch Coppice
Industrial Est

2

00

Trinity Rd

3

Penmire
Brook

Freasley

The Green

4

Overhouse
Farm

2.99

5

Lower

Hill

Delves
Farm

**Edge
Hill**

Evergiade
Road

24

E

Sherwood
CI

F

PO

Pinewood

St Smith Church

Boulters

Delves Crs

G Lane

H

**Wood
End**

Tamwort

The Alders	40 D3
Alvecote	43 G3
Amington	42 C5
Belgrave	46 B3
Birchmoor	47 H5
Bitterscote	4 D7
Blackfords	15 F3
Bolehall	5 H3
Boley Park	32 D2
Bonehill	44 D3
Boney Hay	18 D5
Borough Park	41 G2
Brereton	9 G2
Breretonhill	9 H4
Bridgetown	24 D2
Brownhills	38 C4
Burntwood	28 C2
Burntwood Green	29 F3
Cannock	14 C3
Cannock Wood	18 A1
Chadsmoor	15 E2
Chase Terrace	28 A1
Chasetown	28 B3
Cheslyn Hay	34 D1
Chorley	19 G4
Churchbridge	25 F4
Church Hill	16 B1
Cold Well	18 D1
Coton	40 B3
Creswell Green	19 G4
Curborough	22 B1
Darnford	3 K7
Darnford	32 D3
Dogingtree Estate	10 D3
Dosthill	49 G2
Drayton Bassett	48 C2
Edge Hill	51 F5
Edial	29 G3
Elmhurst	21 G1
Etchinghill	6 B3
Farewell	20 A2
Fazeley	45 F3
Freasley	51 F3
Gentleshaw	18 C2
Gillway	41 F2
Glascote	5 J7
Goosemoor Green	19 E1
Gorsley Ley	29 E2
Great Wyrley	35 G1
Green Heath	11 G4
Hammerwich	29 F5
Hawks Green	15 G5
Hayfield Hill	18 B2
Hazelslade	13 E5
Heath Hayes	16 D5
Hednesford	12 A5
High Town	15 F1
Hilliard's Cross	23 H1
Hobble End	36 A5
Hockley	50 B2
Huddlesford	33 G1
Huntington	10 D5
Kettlebrook	4 E7
Landywood	35 E2
Laney Green	34 A2
Leamonsley	31 E2
Leyfields	41 E3
The Leys	4 B2
Lichfield	2 A4
Little Norton	37 F2
Littlewood	24 D5
Littleworth	16 D2
Little Wyrley	36 B4
Middle Hill	24 A5
Mile Oak	44 C3
Nether Stowe	22 B4
New Town	38 D2
Norton Canes	26 C4
Norton East	27 E3
Norton Green	26 C5
Oldfallow	14 C3
Perry Crofts	41 H2
Pipehill	30 B4
Prospect Village	17 F2
Pye Green	
Quarry Hill	
Rawnsley	
Rugeley	
Rumer Hill	
Sandfields	
Shuttington	
Slitting Mill	
Springhill	
Stoneydelph	
Stonywell	
Stowe	
Streethay	
Summerhill	
Tamworth	
Triangle	
Two Gates	
Upper Landywood	
Warstone	
West Chadsmoor	
West Hill	
Whateley	
Wilnecote	
Wimblebury	
Woodhouses	

USING THE STREET INDEX

Street names are listed alphabetically. Each street name is followed by its postal town or area locality, the Postcode District, the page number, and the reference to the square in which the name is found.

Standard index entries are shown as follows:

Abbey Rd *TAM/AM/WIL* B77 ....**5** J7

Street names and selected addresses not shown on the map due to scale restrictions are shown in the index with an asterisk:

Allton Ct *TAM/AM/WIL* * B77 ....**46** B1

GENERAL ABBREVIATIONS

ACC	ACCESS	DRY	DRIVEWAY	KG	KING	PT	
ALY	ALLEY	DWGS	DWELLINGS	KNL	KNOLL	PTH	
AP	APPROACH	E	EAST	L	LAKE	PZ	
AR	ARCADE	EMB	EMBANKMENT	LA	LANE	QD	QUA
ASS	ASSOCIATION	EMBY	EMBASSY	LDG	LODGE	QU	
AV	AVENUE	ESP	ESPLANADE	LGT	LIGHT	QY	
BCH	BEACH	EST	ESTATE	LK	LOCK	R	
BLDS	BUILDINGS	EX	EXCHANGE	LKS	LAKES	RBT	ROUN
BND	BEND	EXPY	EXPRESSWAY	LNDG	LANDING	RD	
BNK	BANK	EXT	EXTENSION	LTL	LITTLE	RDG	
BR	BRIDGE	F/O	FLYOVER	LWR	LOWER	REP	RE
BRK	BROOK	FC	FOOTBALL CLUB	MAG	MAGISTRATE	RES	RES
BTM	BOTTOM	FK	FORK	MAN	MANSIONS	RFC	RUGBY FOOTBA
BUS	BUSINESS	FLD	FIELD	MD	MEAD	RI	
BVD	BOULEVARD	FLDS	FIELDS	MDW	MEADOWS	RP	
BY	BYPASS	FLS	FALLS	MEM	MEMORIAL	RW	
CATH	CATHEDRAL	FLS	FLATS	MKT	MARKET	S	
CEM	CEMETERY	FM	FARM	MKTS	MARKETS	SCH	S
CEN	CENTRE	FT	FORT	ML	MALL	SE	SOUT
CFT	CROFT	FWY	FREEWAY	ML	MILL	SER	SERVIC
CH	CHURCH	FY	FERRY	MNR	MANOR	SH	
CHA	CHASE	GA	GATE	MS	MEWS	SHOP	SH
CHYD	CHURCHYARD	GAL	GALLERY	MSN	MISSION	SKWY	S
CIR	CIRCLE	GDN	GARDEN	MT	MOUNT	SMT	S
CIRC	CIRCUS	GDNS	GARDENS	MTN	MOUNTAIN	SOC	S
CL	CLOSE	GLD	GLADE	MTS	MOUNTAINS	SP	
CLFS	CLIFFS	GLN	GLEN	MUS	MUSEUM	SPR	
CMP	CAMP	GN	GREEN	MWY	MOTORWAY	SQ	
CNR	CORNER	GND	GROUND	N	NORTH	ST	
CO	COUNTY	GRA	GRANGE	NE	NORTH EAST	STN	S
COLL	COLLEGE	GRG	GARAGE	NW	NORTH WEST	STR	S
COM	COMMON	GT	GREAT	O/P	OVERPASS	STRD	S
COMM	COMMISSION	GTWY	GATEWAY	OFF	OFFICE	SW	SOUT
CON	CONVENT	GV	GROVE	ORCH	ORCHARD	TDG	T
COT	COTTAGE	HGR	HIGHER	OV	OVAL	TER	TE
COTS	COTTAGES	HL	HILL	PAL	PALACE	THWY	THROU
CP	CAPE	HLS	HILLS	PAS	PASSAGE	TNL	T
CPS	COPSE	HO	HOUSE	PAV	PAVILION	TOLL	TO
CR	CREEK	HOL	HOLLOW	PDE	PARADE	TPK	TU
CREM	CREMATORIUM	HOSP	HOSPITAL	PH	PUBLIC HOUSE	TR	
CRS	CRESCENT	HRB	HARBOUR	PK	PARK	TRL	
CSWY	CAUSEWAY	HTH	HEATH	PKWY	PARKWAY	TWR	
CT	COURT	HTS	HEIGHTS	PL	PLACE	U/P	UND
CTRL	CENTRAL	HVN	HAVEN	PLN	PLAIN	UNI	UNIV
CTS	COURTS	HWY	HIGHWAY	PLNS	PLAINS	UPR	
CTYD	COURTYARD	IMP	IMPERIAL	PLZ	PLAZA	V	
CUTT	CUTTINGS	IN	INLET	POL	POLICE STATION	VA	
CV	COVE	IND EST	INDUSTRIAL ESTATE	PR	PRINCE	VIAD	V
CYN	CANYON	INF	INFIRMARY	PREC	PRECINCT	VIL	
DEPT	DEPARTMENT	INFO	INFORMATION	PREP	PREPARATORY	VIS	
DL	DALE	INT	INTERCHANGE	PRIM	PRIMARY	VLG	
DM	DAM	IS	ISLAND	PROM	PROMENADE	VLS	
DR	DRIVE	JCT	JUNCTION	PRS	PRINCESS	VW	
DRO	DROVE	JTY	JETTY	PRT	PORT	W	

.....WOOD	WK .....WALK	WLS .....WELLS	YD .....YARD
.....WHARF	WKS .....WALKS	WY .....WAY	YHA.....YOUTH HOSTEL

CODE TOWNS AND AREA ABBREVIATIONS

- .....Aldridge
- .....Atherstone
- .....Bloxwich/Pelsall
- .....Burntwood
- .....Brownhills

- CNCK/NC .....Cannock/Norton Canes
- CRTAM .....Central & Rural Tamworth
- GTWY .....Great Wyrley
- HEDN .....Hednesford
- LICH .....Lichfield

- LICHS.....Lichfield south
- PENK .....Penkridge
- POL/KGSB/FAZ.....Polesworth/Kingsbury/Fazeley
- RUGE .....Rugeley

- TAM/AM/WIL .....Tamworth/Amington/Wilnecote
- WNSFLD .....Wednesfield
- WOLVN.....Wolverhampton north

ex - streets

Abb - Blu

A (left column, cropped)

- TAM/AM/WIL B77.....5 J7
- HEDN WS12.....11 H4
- d CNCK/NC WS11.....15 E1
- rd Rd LICHS WS14.....3 H4
- k RUGE WS15.....9 H3
- M/AM/WIL B77.....46 C1
- t LICH WS13.....21 F5
- LICH WS13.....30 C1
- I GTWY WS6.....35 F3
- NTWD WS7.....18 C5
- C WS11.....16 A4
- S6.....35 G3
- Cl CNCK/NC WS11.....14 B5
- l CNCK/NC WS11.....15 E1
- CRTAM B79.....41 H3
- POL/KGSB/FAZ B78.....44 C3
- HEDN WS12.....12 D5
- POL/KGSB/FAZ B78.....45 F3
- WS6.....35 F3
- l GTWY WS6.....34 D2
- HEDN WS12.....16 C3
- S6.....6 C2
- vie Dr HEDN WS12.....16 C2
- CRTAM B79.....5 F2
- SB/FAZ B78.....45 F4
- CNCK/NC WS11.....15 E2
- S12.....16 B1
- CNCK/NC WS11.....15 E2
- BRWNH WS8.....38 A4
- CRTAM B79.....5 G2
- S15.....7 E4
- d CNCK/NC WS11.....37 E1
- st BNTWD WS7.....28 B1
- CHS WS14.....32 D2
- CRTAM B79.....13 E5
- OL/KGSB/FAZ B78.....44 D2
- M Ms CRTAM B79.....5 C3
- V S12.....6 F2
- HEDN WS12.....13 E5
- OL/KGSB/FAZ B78.....44 D2
- TAM/AM/WIL B77.....46 D2
- l CNCK/NC WS11.....16 A4
- d HEDN WS12.....10 D3
- l HEDN WS12.....16 B2
- GTWY WS6.....35 G4
- HEDN WS12.....16 B2
- HEDN WS12.....16 B2
- CNCK/NC WS11.....14 B5
- Cl TAM/AM/WIL * B77.....49 H3
- RTAM B79.....41 E2
- M/AM/WIL B77.....46 B5
- GTWY WS6.....35 F1
- TAM/AM/WIL B77.....47 E1
- HEDN WS12.....16 A4
- e TAM/AM/WIL B77.....47 F3
- l Rd TAM/AM/WIL B77.....5 H4
- TAM/AM/WIL B77.....42 B5
- CRTAM B79.....4 C1
- Pl CNCK/NC WS11.....15 G2
- levan Pl RUGE WS15.....6 D3
- BNTWD WS7.....18 A5
- TAM/AM/WIL B77.....46 C1
- Cl BNTWD WS7.....28 B5
- Crs BRWNH WS8.....38 B2
- hmere HEDN WS12.....16 A1
- Rd BRWNH WS8.....38 B2
- 13.....21 H4
- St HEDN WS12.....15 H1
- CNCK/NC WS11.....14 D3
- Cl LICH WS13.....31 F2
- BNTWD WS7.....29 F3

- Ankerdrive CRTAM B79.....5 F4
- Anker Vw TAM/AM/WIL B77.....5 C6
- Ann Crs CNCK/NC WS11.....11 E5
- Anson Av LICH WS13.....2 B2
- Anson Cl BNTWD WS7.....29 E2
- GTWY WS6.....35 F3
- Anson Rd GTWY WS6.....35 F3
- Anson St RUGE WS15.....7 E4
- Anstree Cl GTWY WS6.....34 D3
- Ansty Dr HEDN WS12.....16 B4
- Antler Dr RUGE WS15.....6 B3
- Apex Rd BRWNH WS8.....37 C5
- Apollo CRTAM B79.....4 A1
- Apollo Cl CNCK/NC WS11.....15 G1
- Appian Cl TAM/AM/WIL B77.....45 H5
- Appledore Cl GTWY WS6.....35 G1
- HEDN WS12.....16 C1
- Apple Wk CNCK/NC WS11.....16 A4
- Arbor Cl TAM/AM/WIL B77.....5 J6
- Arbour Ms CNCK/NC * WS11.....26 D3
- Arch St RUGE WS15.....7 F5
- Arden Cl RUGE WS15.....6 C4
- Arden Rd TAM/AM/WIL B77.....50 C2
- Ardgay Dr HEDN WS12.....11 F4
- Argyle Av GTWY WS6.....5 J4
- Argyle St TAM/AM/WIL B77.....46 B1
- Ariane CRTAM B79.....40 D2
- Arion Cl TAM/AM/WIL B77.....5 K2
- Arkall Cl CRTAM B79.....41 H2
- Arkle Cl TAM/AM/WIL B77.....49 H3
- Armishaw Pl RUGE WS15.....9 H3
- Armitage Gdns RUGE WS15.....9 H2
- Armitage La RUGE WS15.....9 H3
- Armitage Rd RUGE WS15.....9 G1
- Armstrong CRTAM B79.....4 B1
- Arnold Cl CRTAM B79.....4 C1
- Arnotdale Dr HEDN WS12.....11 F4
- Arran Cl CNCK/NC WS11.....15 G3
- Arran Dr TAM/AM/WIL B77.....46 C5
- Arthur Evans Cl RUGE * WS15.....9 G3
- Arthur St LICH WS13.....15 F2
- HEDN WS12.....16 C3
- Arundel TAM/AM/WIL B77.....45 H5
- Ascot Cl LICHS WS14.....3 H5
- Ascot Dr CNCK/NC WS11.....24 B1
- TAM/AM/WIL B77.....49 H3
- Ashbourne Cl CNCK/NC WS11.....15 G2
- Ashby Rd CRTAM B79.....41 H2
- Ashdale Cl HEDN WS12.....10 C4
- Ashdale Rd TAM/AM/WIL B77.....5 K3
- Ashgrove BNTWD WS7.....28 B4
- Ash Gv CNCK/NC WS11.....15 F2
- LICH WS13.....3 J2
- TAM/AM/WIL B77.....50 C2
- Ashlands Cl CRTAM B79.....41 H2
- Ash La GTWY WS6.....35 G1
- Ashleigh Dr TAM/AM/WIL B77.....46 B4
- Ashleigh Rd RUGE WS15.....9 E1
- Ashley Rd BNTWD WS7.....17 H5
- Ashmall HEDN WS7.....29 F5
- Ashmead Rd BNTWD WS7.....28 C1
- Ashmole Cl LICHS WS14.....3 J7
- Ashtree Bank RUGE WS15.....9 E2
- Ash Tree La LICH WS13.....23 E5
- Ash Vw HEDN WS12.....10 D3
- Aspen Cl HEDN WS12.....13 E5
- Aspen Gv BNTWD WS7.....28 B1
- Asquith Dr CNCK/NC WS11.....16 A4
- Athelstan Wy CRTAM B79.....41 E2
- Atherstone Pl POL/KGSB/FAZ B78.....45 G4
- Attingham Dr CNCK/NC WS11.....15 H5
- Attlee Crs RUGE WS15.....9 F1
- Attlee Gv CNCK/NC WS11.....16 A4
- Attwood Rd BNTWD WS7.....27 G2
- Auchinleck Dr LICH WS13.....22 A5
- Austin Cote La LICHS WS14.....3 K4
- Autumn Dr LICH WS13.....22 A4
- Avenue Rd HEDN WS12.....16 C4
- Averill Dr RUGE WS15.....6 D3
- Avill TAM/AM/WIL B77.....50 D2

- Avon TAM/AM/WIL B77.....50 D2
- Avonlea Gdns RUGE WS15.....6 C4
- Avon Rd BNTWD WS7.....28 B4
- CNCK/NC WS11.....24 D2

B

- Backcester La LICH WS13.....2 D3
- Backcrofts CNCK/NC WS11.....15 E5
- Back La LICHS WS14.....33 H4
- Badger Cl HEDN WS12.....10 C5
- Badgers Wy HEDN WS12.....16 B5
- Bailey Av TAM/AM/WIL B77.....50 C2
- Bailey Cl CNCK/NC WS11.....15 G2
- Baker's La LICH WS13.....2 D4
- Baker St BNTWD WS7.....28 B3
- Baldwin Gv CNCK/NC WS11.....16 A4
- Balfour CRTAM B79.....4 D4
- Balmoral Cl CRTAM B79.....41 G2
- LICHS WS14.....3 H6
- Balmoral Dr HEDN WS12.....11 F4
- Baltic Cl HEDN WS12.....15 E4
- Bamburgh TAM/AM/WIL B77.....45 H5
- Bamford St TAM/AM/WIL B77.....5 K7
- Bampton Av BNTWD WS7.....28 C1
- Banbury Rd CNCK/NC WS11.....24 B1
- Bancroft TAM/AM/WIL B77.....46 C1
- Bank Crs BNTWD WS7.....28 B4
- Bank St HEDN WS12.....16 C5
- Bank Top RUGE WS15.....6 D4
- Barbara St CRTAM B79.....4 D2
- Barber Cl HEDN WS12.....16 C4
- Barcliff Av TAM/AM/WIL B77.....46 B1
- Bardell Cl LICH WS13.....31 E3
- Barlow Cl TAM/AM/WIL B77.....42 B5
- Barnard Wy CNCK/NC WS11.....15 F4
- Barnbridge TAM/AM/WIL B77.....45 H2
- Barn Cl LICH WS13.....21 H3
- RUGE WS15.....9 H3
- Barn Cft BNTWD WS7.....28 C5
- GTWY WS6.....35 G1
- Barnetts La BRWNH WS8.....38 B4
- Barnfield Cl LICHS WS14.....2 D6
- Barnfield Wy HEDN WS12.....13 E5
- Barnswood Cl CNCK/NC WS11.....24 B1
- Baron Cl BNTWD WS7.....18 A5
- Barracks La BRWNH WS8.....39 E5
- Basin La TAM/AM/WIL B77.....5 J6
- Baskeyfield Cl LICHS WS14.....3 K7
- Bateway RUGE WS15.....9 H4
- Bath Rd CNCK/NC WS11.....15 E1
- Bayswater Rd RUGE * WS15.....6 D4
- Beaconfields LICH WS13.....2 A3
- Beacon St LICH WS13.....2 A1
- Beacon Wy HEDN WS12.....16 D3
- Beauchamp Rd TAM/AM/WIL B77.....50 C2
- Beau Ct CNCK/NC WS11.....15 E5
- Beaudesert BNTWD WS7.....18 C5
- Beaudesert Vw HEDN WS12.....17 E1
- Beaumont Cl GTWY WS6.....35 F3
- Beaumont Rd GTWY WS6.....35 F2
- Bedford Pl HEDN WS12.....15 H2
- Beech Av TAM/AM/WIL B77.....46 B1
- Beech Ct GTWY * WS6.....25 C5
- HEDN * WS12.....11 H4
- Beech Crs BNTWD WS7.....28 B3
- Beechen Gv BNTWD WS7.....28 B1
- The Beeches RUGE WS15.....6 B1
- Beeches Rd RUGE WS15.....9 F2
- Beechfield Ri LICH WS13.....3 G3
- Beech Gdns LICHS WS14.....2 E6
- Beech Gv HEDN WS12.....10 D3
- Beechmere Ri RUGE WS15.....6 B3
- Beech Pine Cl HEDN WS12.....11 G3
- Beech Rd CRTAM B79.....41 F1
- Beech Tree La CNCK/NC WS11.....24 D1
- Beechwood Crs TAM/AM/WIL B77.....42 C4

- Beecroft Av LICH WS13.....2 B1
- Beecroft Rd CNCK/NC WS11.....15 E5
- Bees La RUGE WS15.....7 E4
- Belgrave Rd TAM/AM/WIL B77.....46 B4
- Bell Cl LICH WS13.....21 F5
- Bellingham TAM/AM/WIL B77.....47 C3
- Bellsize Cl CNCK/NC WS11.....26 D4
- Bells La BNTWD WS7.....18 B5
- Belmont Av CNCK/NC WS11.....14 C4
- Belmont Cl GTWY WS6.....25 C5
- Belmont Rd TAM/AM/WIL B77.....50 B1
- Belsize TAM/AM/WIL B77.....46 B2
- Belt Rd HEDN WS12.....15 G1
- Belvedere Cl BNTWD WS7.....28 B4
- CRTAM B79.....41 H2
- Belvoir TAM/AM/WIL B77.....45 H5
- Benches Cl BNTWD WS7.....27 H3
- Benion Rd CNCK/NC WS11.....15 F2
- Benson Cl LICH WS13.....3 C1
- Benson Vw CRTAM B79.....41 H1
- Bentley Brook La HEDN WS12.....13 E5
- Bentley Wy CRTAM B79.....41 E2
- Benton's La GTWY WS6.....35 G3
- Berry Hl HEDN WS12.....16 A2
- Berwick Dr CNCK/NC WS11.....24 B1
- Berwyn Gv GTWY WS6.....35 F1
- Besom Wy GTWY WS6.....34 C2
- Betty's La CNCK/NC WS11.....27 E5
- Bevan Lee Rd CNCK/NC WS11.....14 D3
- Beverley Hl HEDN WS12.....12 B5
- Bexmore Dr LICH WS13.....22 D5
- Beyer Cl TAM/AM/WIL B77.....46 D2
- Biddulph Pk BNTWD * WS7.....17 H5
- Bideford Wy CNCK/NC WS11.....24 B1
- Bilberry Cl RUGE WS15.....6 C4
- Bilberry Crs HEDN WS12.....14 C1
- Birch Av BNTWD WS7.....28 B3
- BRWNH WS8.....38 A4
- CNCK/NC WS11.....24 C1
- Birchfields Dr HEDN WS12.....16 B5
- Birch Gv LICH WS13.....3 H3
- POL/KGSB/FAZ B78.....47 C5
- Birch La RUGE WS15.....9 F3
- Birchmoor Rd POL/KGSB/FAZ B78.....47 H4
- Birch Ter BNTWD WS7.....18 C5
- Birchtree La RUGE WS15.....9 E2
- Birchwood Rd LICHS WS14.....3 K5
- Birds Bush Rd TAM/AM/WIL B77.....46 B4
- Bird St LICH WS13.....2 A2
- Birmingham Rd LICH WS13.....2 C6
- LICHS WS14.....31 C4
- Bishops Gra RUGE WS15.....7 F3
- Bitterscote La POL/KGSB/FAZ B78.....45 F2
- Blackdown TAM/AM/WIL B77.....47 F3
- Blackfriars Cl CRTAM B79.....40 D4
- Blackroot Cl BNTWD WS7.....29 F5
- Blackthorn Av BNTWD WS7.....28 B5
- Blackthorn Crs HEDN WS12.....13 E5
- Blackthorne Rd LICHS WS14.....3 G4
- Blackwood Rd TAM/AM/WIL B77.....45 H5
- Blake Cl CNCK/NC WS11.....15 G1
- Blandford Gdns BNTWD WS7.....29 E3
- Bleak House Dr BNTWD WS7.....27 H1
- Blenheim Cl TAM/AM/WIL B77.....5 H5
- Blenheim Rd BNTWD WS7.....28 C1
- CNCK/NC WS11.....27 F5
- Blenheim Wy LICH WS13.....23 F1
- Bletchley Dr TAM/AM/WIL B77.....45 H4
- Blewitt St HEDN WS12.....11 H5
- Blithbury Rd HEDN WS12.....7 H2
- Blithfield Pl CNCK/NC WS11.....15 H5
- Blithfield Rd BRWNH WS8.....37 G2
- Bloomfield Crs LICH WS13.....21 C4
- Bloomfield Wy CRTAM B79.....41 E2
- Bloomsbury Wy LICHS WS14.....3 J4
- Bluebell Cl HEDN WS12.....11 H5
- Bluebell La GTWY WS6.....35 F3

Bluebird Cl *LICHS* WS14 ....3 H3
Blythe Cl *BNTWD* WS7 ....29 F3
Blythe St *TAM/AM/WIL* B77 ....5 H6
Boat La *LICHS* WS14 ....39 H3
Bolebridge St *CRTAM* B79 ....5 F3
Boley Cl *LICHS* WS14 ....3 F5
Boley Cottage La *LICHS* WS14 ....3 H5
Boley La *LICHS* WS14 ....3 G4
Boleyn Cl *GTWY* WS6 ....34 D2
Bondway *HEDN* WS12 ....11 F3
Bonehill Rd *POL/KGSB/FAZ* B78.......4 B5
Boney Hay Rd *BNTWD* WS7 ....28 D1
Booth Cl *LICH* WS13 ....21 G4
Booth St *HEDN* WS12 ....11 H5
Bore St *LICH* WS13 ....2 C4
Borman *CRTAM* B79 ....4 B2
Borough Rd *CRTAM* B79 ....41 G2
Borrowcop La *LICHS* WS14 ....32 A4
Boston Cl *HEDN* WS12 ....16 C5
Boswell Rd *CNCK/NC* WS11 ....14 D2
Boulton Cl *BNTWD* WS7 ....28 D1
Bourne Av *POL/KGSB/FAZ* B78.......44 D4
Bourne Cl *HEDN* WS12 ....16 B4
Bower Cl *LICH* WS13 ....22 B4
Bower La *RUGE* WS15 ....6 B3
Bowes Dr *CNCK/NC* WS11 ....15 F2
Bowling Green Av
  TAM/AM/WIL B77 ....46 B5
Bow St *RUGE* WS15 ....7 E4
Boyden Cl *CNCK/NC* WS11 ....14 B5
Bracken Cl *BNTWD* WS7 ....29 E2
  HEDN WS12 ....12 A3
  LICHS WS14 ....J6
Brackenhill Rd *BNTWD* WS7 ....28 C1
Bracken Rd *HEDN* WS12 ....14 C1
Bracken Wy *RUGE* WS15 ....6 C3
Bracklesham Wy
  TAM/AM/WIL B77 ....42 D3
Bradbury La *HEDN* WS12 ....11 G3
Bradford Rd *BRWNH* WS8 ....38 A4
Bradford St *CNCK/NC* WS11 ....15 C1
  CRTAM B79 ....4 A3
Bradwell La *RUGE* WS15 ....18 B1
Braeburn Cl *LICH* WS13 ....3 H1
Braemar Gdns *HEDN* WS12 ....11 F4
Braemar Rd *CNCK/NC* WS11 ....27 E5
Braham *CRTAM* B79..............40 C3
Brain St *TAM/AM/WIL* B77 ....50 C1
Bramble Cl *HEDN* WS12 ....12 A4
Bramble La *BNTWD* WS7 ....28 D1
Bramble Wy *RUGE* WS15 ....6 C4
The Brambles *LICHS* WS14 ....3 C6
Brambling *TAM/AM/WIL* B77 ....46 D5
Bramley Wy *LICHS* WS14...........33 H4
Brampton Dr *HEDN* WS12 ....6 D4
Bramwell Dr *GTWY* WS6 ....34 D4
Brancaster Cl *TAM/AM/WIL* B77 ...42 D3
Bransdale Rd *BRWNH* WS8.........38 A5
Brantwood Av *BNTWD* WS7 ....28 C4
Breadmarket St *LICH* WS13 ....2 C3
Bream *TAM/AM/WIL* B77 ....46 A5
Breeze Av *CNCK/NC* WS11 ....27 F4
Brendon *TAM/AM/WIL* B77 ....47 E3
Brent *TAM/AM/WIL* B77 ....46 B5
Brereton Manor Ct *RUGE* WS15 ....9 H3
Brewery St *RUGE* WS15 ....7 E5
Brewhouse Ct *LICH* * WS13 ....21 F5
Brewster Ct *POL/KGSB/FAZ* B78 ...44 D3
Briar *TAM/AM/WIL* B77 ....46 D1
Briar Cl *HEDN* WS12 ....11 G3
  RUGE WS15 ....6 C4
Briars Wy *LICHS* WS14...........17 G2
Bricklin St *BRWNH* WS8 ....38 B5
Brick Kiln Wy *RUGE* WS15...........9 F4
Brickworks Rd *HEDN* WS12 ....16 B3
Bridge Av *GTWY* WS6 ....25 K4
Bridge Cross Rd *BNTWD* WS7 ......28 C2
Bridges Crs *CNCK/NC* WS11 ....26 D4
Bridgeside Rd *TAM/AM/WIL* B77 ...45 H2
Bridges Rd *CNCK/NC* WS11 ....26 D4
Bridge St *CNCK/NC* WS11 ....25 E4
  TAM/AM/WIL B77 ....42 B4
Bridgewater St
  TAM/AM/WIL B77 ....5 K3
Bridle Wk *RUGE* WS15 ....6 B3
Briertey Hill La *RUGE* WS15 ....18 D2
Bright Crs *TAM/AM/WIL* B77 ....45 H2
Brindley Bank Rd *RUGE* WS15 ....7 E2
Brindley Crs *HEDN* WS12 ....12 A4
Brindley Heath Rd *HEDN* WS12 ....12 A4
Brindley Rd *HEDN* WS12 ....11 F2
Brinkburn Cl *RUGE* WS15 ....6 B4
Brisbane Wy *HEDN* WS12 ....16 C3
Bristol Cl *CNCK/NC* WS11 ....15 H5
Britannia Wy *LICHS* WS14...........3 K3
Broadhurst Green Rd
  HEDN WS12 ....10 D1
Broadlands Ri *LICHS* WS14...........3 G5

Broad La *LICH* WS13...............30 B4
  LICH WS13 ....33 G1
  LICHS WS14 ....3 G5
Broadlee *TAM/AM/WIL* B77 ....47 F3
Broad Meadow La *GTWY* WS6 .....35 G2
Broadoaks Cl *CNCK/NC* WS11......26 D3
Broadsmeath *TAM/AM/WIL* B77 ...45 H2
Broad St *CNCK/NC* WS11...........25 E3
Broadway *HEDN* WS12 ....11 F5
Bromley Cl *HEDN* WS12 ....11 H4
Bronte Cl *CRTAM* B79 ....41 F3
Bronte Dr *CNCK/NC* WS11..........16 A4
Brook Av *TAM/AM/WIL* B77 ....46 C5
Brook Cl *LICH* WS13...............2 B1
Brook End *BNTWD* WS7 ....28 C5
  POL/KGSB/FAZ B78...............45 H4
Brooke Rd *HEDN* WS12 ....11 F5
Brookfield Dr *CNCK/NC* WS11 ....25 E2
Brookhay La *LICH* WS13 ....23 H2
Brooklands Av *GTWY* WS6...........5 G1
Brooklands Rd *CNCK/NC* WS11 ....15 G2
Brook La *GTWY* WS6 ....35 G1
Brooklyn Rd *BNTWD* WS7 ....28 C5
  HEDN WS12 ....16 B5
Brook Rd *GTWY* WS6 ....25 E4
Brookside Rd
  POL/KGSB/FAZ B78...............44 C3
Brookside Wy *TAM/AM/WIL* B77...50 C1
Brook V *CNCK/NC* WS11...........25 F1
Brookweed *TAM/AM/WIL* B77 ....46 D1
Broomhill Bank *CNCK/NC* WS11 ...15 E3
Broomhill Cl *CNCK/NC* WS11 ....15 C2
Brownhills Rd *CNCK/NC* WS11 .....27 F4
Browning Cl *CRTAM* B79...........40 D1
Browning Rd *BNTWD* WS7 ....29 E2
Brownsfield Rd *LICH* WS13...........3 F1
Browns *CRTAM* B79 ....41 H1
Browsholme *CRTAM* B79 ....40 C3
Brunel Cl *BNTWD* WS7 ....28 D1
  CRTAM B79 ....4 D1
Brunswick Rd *CNCK/NC* WS11 .....15 E4
Bryans La *RUGE* WS15...............7 F4
Bryans Wy *HEDN* WS12 ....16 D2
Buckden *TAM/AM/WIL* B77 ....47 F3
Buckingham Gdns *LICHS* * WS14....2 D7
Buckingham Pl *HEDN* WS12........16 A5
Buckingham Rd *CRTAM* B79........40 C2
Buckland Cl *HEDN* WS12 ....16 B5
Buckthorn Cl *HEDN* WS12...........11 F3
Buds Rd *RUGE* WS15 ....18 B1
Bulldog La *LICH* WS13...............2 C1
Bungalows *GTWY* * WS6...........35 G3
Bunyan Pl *CNCK/NC* WS11 ....15 E2
Burdock Cl *HEDN* WS12 ....15 H3
Burgoyne St *CNCK/NC* WS11 ....15 G1
Burleigh Cl *HEDN* WS12 ....11 G3
Burleigh Cft *BNTWD* WS7 ....29 E5
Burnfield Dr *RUGE* WS15 ....6 C4
Burnham Gn *CNCK/NC* WS11 ....24 B1
Burns Cl *LICHS* WS14...............2 C7
Burns Dr *BNTWD* WS7 ....29 E2
Burns Rd *CRTAM* B79 ....41 F3
Burns St *CNCK/NC* WS11...........15 G2
Burnthill La *RUGE* WS15 ....9 E1
Burntwood Rd *BNTWD* WS7 ....29 F5
  CNCK/NC WS11 ....27 E3
Burton Cl *CRTAM* B79...............41 H2
Burton Old Rd *LICH* WS13...........22 D5
  LICHS WS14 ....32 D1
Burton Old Rd East *LICHS* WS14 ...3 J3
Burton Old Rd West *LICH* WS13.....3 H4
Burton Rd *LICH* WS13...............22 D5
Bush Dr *RUGE* WS15...............7 E4
Buttermere Cl *TAM/AM/WIL* B77...47 E5
Buttermere Dr *CNCK/NC* WS11 ....15 G3
Butts Cl *CNCK/NC* WS11...........26 C5
Butts La *CNCK/NC* WS11...........26 C5
Buxton Av *POL/KGSB/FAZ* B78.....45 G4
Byland Cl *TAM/AM/WIL* B77 ....5 K6
By Pass Rd *TAM/AM/WIL* B77 ......42 D4
Byron Av *LICHS* WS14...............31 H4
Byron Cl *BNTWD* WS7 ....18 B5
Byron Pl *CNCK/NC* WS11...........15 F1
  RUGE WS15 ....6 C3
Byron Rd *CRTAM* B79 ....41 F2

C

Cadman's La *GTWY* WS6 ....36 A4
Cadogan Rd *TAM/AM/WIL* B77 .....50 A2
Caister Cl *HEDN* WS12...............16 D4
Caistor Cl *POL/KGSB/FAZ* B78 .....44 A4
Calder *TAM/AM/WIL* B77...........47 E2
Cale Cl *TAM/AM/WIL* B77...........45 H2
Caledonian *TAM/AM/WIL* B77 ......46 C2
Californian Gv *BNTWD* WS7 ....28 B1

Callaghan Gv *CNCK/NC* WS11......16 A4
Calving Hl *CNCK/NC* WS11...........15 E4
Cambrian *TAM/AM/WIL* B77.........46 C2
Cambrian La *RUGE* WS15 ....6 C2
Cambria St *CNCK/NC* WS11 ....14 D3
Camden Dr *TAM/AM/WIL* B77 ......46 B1
Camelot Cl *CNCK/NC* WS11.........15 F2
Camhouses *TAM/AM/WIL* B77......47 E2
Campbell Cl *CRTAM* B79...........41 E1
  RUGE WS15 ....6 D3
Campian's Av *GTWY* WS6...........34 D2
Campion Dr *TAM/AM/WIL* B77......5 G7
Camsey La *BNTWD* WS7 ....29 E3
Canaway Wk *RUGE* WS15...........6 C3
Canford Pl *CNCK/NC* * WS11 ....15 F5
Cannel Rd *BNTWD* WS7 ....27 H2
Canning Rd *TAM/AM/WIL* B77......42 B5
Cannock Rd *BNTWD* WS7...........28 B2
  CNCK/NC WS11 ....15 F3
  CNCK/NC WS11 ....15 F3
Cannock Wood Rd *HEDN* WS12....17 F1
Cannock Wood St *HEDN* WS12 ....13 G5
Canterbury Cl *TAM/AM/WIL* B77....5 J6
Canterbury Dr *BNTWD* WS7 ....5 G7
Canterbury Wy *CNCK/NC* WS11....15 H5
Cappers La *LICHS* WS14...............3 K3
  LICHS WS14 ....33 E2
Caradoc *TAM/AM/WIL* B77 ....46 D2
Cardigan Av *RUGE* WS15...........8 D2
Cardigan Pl *HEDN* WS12 ....16 A1
Cardinal Wy *CNCK/NC* WS11.......14 D4
Carey *TAM/AM/WIL* B77...........50 D2
Carfax *CNCK/NC* WS11...........25 E1
Carisbrooke *TAM/AM/WIL* B77......46 D2
Carlcroft *TAM/AM/WIL* B77 ....47 E2
Carlisle Rd *CNCK/NC* WS11 ....24 B2
Carlton Cl *HEDN* WS12 ....16 B5
Carlton Crs *BNTWD* WS7 ....28 C1
  CRTAM B79 ....41 E1
Carmel Cl *HEDN* WS12 ....16 A1
Carmichael Cl *LICHS* WS14...........3 C5
Carnoustie *TAM/AM/WIL* B77 ......43 E4
Castle Cl *BRWNH* WS8...............38 B2
  TAM/AM/WIL B77 ....42 B5
Castlecroft *CNCK/NC* WS11.........26 C4
Castle Dyke *LICH* WS13...............2 D4
Castlehall *TAM/AM/WIL* B77........46 D2
Castle Rd *TAM/AM/WIL* B77........50 C2
Castle St *BRWNH* WS8...............38 B2
Castle Vw *TAM/AM/WIL* B77.........5 G6
Cathedral Ri *LICH* WS13...............2 B2
Catkin Wk *RUGE* WS15 ....6 C3
Catshill Rd *BRWNH* WS8...........38 C5
Cavan's Cl *CNCK/NC* WS11 ....15 E2
Cavell Rd *BNTWD* WS7...........29 C1
Cavendish *CRTAM* B79...........40 D1
Caxton St *CNCK/NC* WS11...........25 E1
Cecil St *CNCK/NC* WS11...........15 F2
Cedar Av *BRWNH* WS8...............38 C4
Cedar Cl *BNTWD* WS7 ....28 C3
  HEDN WS12 ....11 G2
  LICHS WS14 ....32 D2
Cedar Crs *RUGE* WS15 ....9 G3
Cedar Dr *CRTAM* B79 ....41 F1
Cedar Gv *GTWY* WS6...............25 H5
Cedarhill Dr *CNCK/NC* WS11.......15 F4
Cedar Rd *BNTWD* WS7...........28 C3
Celandine *TAM/AM/WIL* B77 ....5 G7
Celtic Rd *CNCK/NC* WS11...........15 E2
Cemetery Rd *CNCK/NC* WS11......14 D2
Cemetery St *GTWY* WS6...........34 D1
Central Av *TAM/AM/WIL* B77 ....51 E1
Centurion Wy *TAM/AM/WIL* B77...51 E1
Chad's Ditch *HEDN* WS12...........11 E1
Chadsfield Rd *RUGE* WS15...........7 E3
Chadwell Hts *LICHS* WS13...........22 B3
Chadwick St *RUGE* WS15...............7 F5
Chaffinch Cl *HEDN* WS12 ....15 H3
Chalcot Dr *HEDN* WS12 ....11 F4
Chalfield *CRTAM* B79...........40 C3
Chalfont Av *CNCK/NC* WS11 ....24 C1
Chancery Dr *HEDN* WS12...........11 E1
Chandlers Dr *TAM/AM/WIL* B77....43 E4
Chapel Av *BRWNH* WS8...........38 A2
Chapel Dr *BRWNH* WS8...........38 A2
Chapel La *LICHS* WS14...............2 D2
  RUGE WS15 ....18 A1
Chapelon *TAM/AM/WIL* B77.........46 D2
Chapel Sq *GTWY* WS6...........34 D1
Chapel St *BNTWD* WS7 ....27 H1
  BRWNH WS8 ....38 A2
  CNCK/NC WS11 ....26 D4
  HEDN WS12 ....16 C5
Chaplain Rd *HEDN* WS12...........16 C4
Charlemonte Cl *HEDN* WS12 ......16 B3
Charles Cl *GTWY* WS6...........34 D3
Charlock Gv *HEDN* WS12...........16 A3
Charnwood Cl *HEDN* WS12.........16 A2

LICH WS13 ....
  RUGE WS15 ....
Charter Cl *CNCK/NC* WS11 ....
Charterfield Dr *HEDN* WS12...............
The Charters *LICH* WS13...............
Chartwell *CRTAM* B79...............
Chase Av *GTWY* WS6...............
Chaselands *BNTWD* WS7...............
Chaseley Av *CNCK/NC* WS11...............
Chaseley Cl *RUGE* WS15...............
Chaseley Cft *CNCK/NC* WS11 ....
Chaseley Gdns *BNTWD* WS7...............
Chaseley Rd *RUGE* WS15...............
The Chase Link *BRWNH* * WS8
Chase Rd *BNTWD* WS7...............
  BRWNH WS8 ....
Chaseside Dr *HEDN* WS12...............
Chase Side Dr *RUGE* WS15...............
Chase V *BNTWD* WS7...............
Chasewater Wy *CNCK/NC* WS11...............
Chatterton Av *LICH* WS13...............
Chaucer Cl *CRTAM* B79...............
  LICHS WS14 ....
Chaucer Dr *BNTWD* WS7...............
Chawner Cl *BNTWD* WS7...............
The Chequers *LICH* * WS13...............
Chequers Ct *CNCK/NC* WS11 ....
Cherrington Dr *GTWY* WS6...............
Cherry Bank *HEDN* WS12...............
Cherry Cl *BNTWD* WS7...............
Cherry Orch *LICHS* WS14...............
Cherry St *CRTAM* B79...............
Cherry Tree Rd *CNCK/NC* WS11
  HEDN WS12 ....
  RUGE WS15 ....
Cherry Tree Wk *CRTAM* B79...............
Cherwell Dr *BRWNH* WS8...............
Cheslyn Dr *GTWY* WS6...............
Chestall Rd *RUGE* WS15...............
Chester Cl *CNCK/NC* WS11 ....
  LICH WS13 ....
Chesterfield Rd *LICHS* WS13...............
Chester Rd North *BRWNH* WS8
Chesterton Wy *CRTAM* B79...............
Chestnut Av *CRTAM* B79...............
Chestnut Cl *CNCK/NC* WS11...............
Chestnut Dr *GTWY* WS6...............
  GTWY WS6 ....
Chetwynd Cl *RUGE* WS15...............
Chetwynd Gdns
  CNCK/NC * WS11 ....
Chetwynd Pk *HEDN* WS12...............
Cheviot *TAM/AM/WIL* B77...............
Cheviot Dr *RUGE* WS15...............
Cheviot Ri *HEDN* WS12...............
Chichester Dr *CNCK/NC* WS11 ....
Chieveley Cl *RUGE* WS15...............
Chillingham *TAM/AM/WIL* B77...............
Chillington Cl *GTWY* WS6...............
Chiltern Cl *GTWY* WS6...............
Chiltern Rd *TAM/AM/WIL* B77...............
Chorley Rd *BNTWD* WS7...............
Christ Church Gdns *LICH* WS13
Christchurch La *LICH* WS13...............
Chub *TAM/AM/WIL* B77...............
Churchbridge Pk
  CNCK/NC * WS11 ....
Church Cl *POL/KGSB/FAZ* B78 ....
  RUGE WS15 ....
Churchcroft Gdns *RUGE* WS15...............
Church Dr *POL/KGSB/FAZ* B78...............
Church Hl *HEDN* WS12...............
Church La *BNTWD* WS7...............
  CRTAM B79 ....
  CRTAM B79 ....
  RUGE WS15 ....
Church Rd *BNTWD* WS7...............
  BRWNH WS8 ....
  CNCK/NC WS11 ....
  CNCK/NC WS11 ....
  TAM/AM/WIL B77 ....
Church St *BNTWD* WS7...............
  CNCK/NC WS11 ....
  CNCK/NC WS11 ....
  CNCK/NC WS11 ....
  CRTAM B79 ....
  LICH WS13 ....
  LICHS WS14 ....
  RUGE WS15 ....
Church V *CNCK/NC* WS11...............
Cinder Rd *BNTWD* WS7...............
City Ar *LICH* WS13...............
Claremont Rd *CRTAM* B79...............
Clarion Wy *CNCK/NC* WS11...............
Clarke's Av *HEDN* WS12...............
Claverdon Cl *BRWNH* WS8...............
Claygate Rd *HEDN* WS12...............
Claymore *TAM/AM/WIL* B77...............

LICHS WS14 ....31 F5
AM/AM/WIL B77 ....47 F3
: HEDN WS12 ....16 B5
M/AM/WIL B77 ....5 K6
AM/AM/WIL B77 ....46 C1
Dr CNCK/NC WS11 ....15 H2
GTWY WS6 ....34 D3
: TAM/AM/WIL B77 ....46 B1
CNCK/NC WS11 ....24 C2
379 ....41 E2
s BNTWD WS7 ....28 D1
NTWD WS7 ....28 C2
LICH WS13 ....2 B2
w HEDN WS12 ....16 A5
g GTWY WS6 ....34 C1
use La RUGE WS15 ....7 E4
RUGE WS15 ....9 G3
Rd RUGE WS15 ....9 H2
Rd BNTWD WS7 ....27 G2
HEDN WS12 ....12 A4
/AM/WIL B77 ....46 A5
Nook RUGE WS15 ....6 C2
row La CNCK/NC WS11 ....14 A2
St POL/KGSB/FAZ B78 ....47 H5
e Rd
SB/FAZ B78 ....45 F2
RTAM B79 ....5 F3
Cl CRTAM B79 ....41 F3
Rd POL/KGSB/FAZ B78 ....45 F5
d Cl GTWY WS6 ....35 F3
CRTAM B79 ....5 F3
M/AM/WIL B77 ....46 D3
BRWNH WS8 ....37 G5
S6 ....34 D2
d RUGE WS15 ....9 F4
LICH WS13 ....21 G4
Cl LICHS WS14 ....3 H5
RUGE WS15 ....7 E1
Vw GTWY WS6 ....35 E2
n Crs BNTWD WS7 ....28 B1
n Dr CNCK/NC WS11 ....15 F3
n Wy CNCK/NC WS11 ....15 F3
rd Rd CRTAM B79 ....41 F1
La CNCK/NC WS11 ....15 G3
* B79 ....5 F4
13 ....23 F1
Side RUGE WS15 ....18 C3
Vw BNTWD WS7 ....18 C5
/S12 ....11 H4
Rd CRTAM B79 ....41 E2
v CNCK/NC WS11 ....16 A5
Rd CNCK/NC WS11 ....27 E5
t LICH WS13 ....2 D3
HEDN WS12 ....11 G3
TAM/AM/WIL B77 ....47 E5
Wy CNCK/NC WS11 ....15 E5
Cl CNCK/NC WS11 ....24 D1
Rd CNCK/NC WS11 ....24 B1
Coppice HEDN * WS12 ....17 F2
CRTAM B79 ....41 F2
elds LICHS WS14 ....3 G4
ns Rd HEDN WS12 ....16 B2
ill Cl HEDN WS12 ....11 F4
ice HEDN WS12 ....16 C5
Cl BNTWD WS7 ....28 B1
/S6 ....24 D5
Ct CNCK/NC * WS11 ....24 B2
Crs BRWNH WS8 ....37 H5
Gv LICHS WS14 ....32 D2
a BRWNH WS8 ....37 H4
C WS11 ....24 D5
Rd RUGE WS15 ....9 E2
Side BRWNH WS8 ....37 H4
ok La BNTWD WS7 ....28 D4
e Av BNTWD WS7 ....28 B5
M/AM/WIL B77 ....42 C5
Dr LICHS WS14 ....3 K4
NCK/NC WS11 ....15 E1
Av POL/KGSB/FAZ B78 ....45 F3
Rd HEDN WS12 ....15 H1
on Av
SB/FAZ B78 ....44 C3
on St CRTAM B79 ....4 D2
ion St CRTAM B79 ....4 E3
TAM/AM/WIL B77 ....47 F3
Cl BNTWD WS7 ....28 B1
Dr HEDN WS12 ....11 G3
NTWD WS7 ....28 D1
CRTAM B79 ....40 C2
Av GTWY WS6 ....35 F1
Rd HEDN WS12 ....11 G3
Cl BNTWD WS7 ....28 B4
VS12 ....16 B2
Farm Rd
M/WIL B77 ....46 A5
La BNTWD WS7 ....28 B4
v HEDN WS12 ....11 G2
Cl BNTWD WS7 ....17 H5

Coulter La *BNTWD* WS7 ....19 G5
Coulthwaite Wy *RUGE* WS15 ....9 F2
County Dr *POL/KGSB/FAZ* B78 ....45 E3
Covey Cl *LICH* WS13 ....3 G1
Cow La *POL/KGSB/FAZ* B78 ....50 C4
Cowley *TAM/AM/WIL* B77 ....46 B2
Cowley Gn *HEDN* WS12 ....11 F3
Crab La *CNCK/NC* WS11 ....15 G3
Crabtree Wy *RUGE* WS15 ....6 C4
Crane Dr *BNTWD* WS7 ....28 C5
Crane Fld *LICH* WS13 ....21 G5
Cranfield Rd *BNTWD* WS7 ....28 C2
Cranleigh Wy *LICHS* WS14 ....3 J4
Cranmer Cl *GTWY* WS6 ....34 C3
Craven *TAM/AM/WIL* B77 ....47 E3
The Crescent *BNTWD* WS7 ....18 B5
GTWY WS6 ....35 G2
Crestwood *TAM/AM/WIL* B77 ....42 D4
Crestwood Ri *RUGE* WS15 ....6 C2
Cricket La *LICHS* WS14 ....32 A5
Crigdon *TAM/AM/WIL* B77 ....47 F3
Cringlebrook *TAM/AM/WIL* B77 ....46 A3
The Croft *GTWY* WS6 ....35 E2
Croft Av *HEDN* WS12 ....11 G2
Croft Crs *BRWNH* WS8 ....37 H5
Croft Gdns *BNTWD* WS7 ....28 C1
Croft St *CRTAM* B79 ....5 F1
Cromdale *TAM/AM/WIL* B77 ....47 F3
Cromwell Rd *CRTAM* B79 ....40 D1
HEDN WS12 ....16 B5
Cromwells Meadow *LICHS* WS14 ....32 A4
Crossfell *TAM/AM/WIL* B77 ....47 E3
Crossfield Rd *LICH* WS13 ....3 K2
The Crossings *LICH* WS13 ....3 J3
Cross in Hand La *LICH* WS13 ....20 A2
Cross Keys *LICH* WS13 ....2 D3
Cross La *LICHS* WS14 ....3 H6
Crossley Stone *RUGE* WS15 ....7 E4
Cross Rd *RUGE* WS15 ....9 E1
Cross St *BNTWD* WS7 ....28 A1
CNCK/NC WS11 ....25 E4
GTWY WS6 ....34 D2
HEDN WS12 ....16 C5
TAM/AM/WIL B77 ....5 G6
Crowden Rd *TAM/AM/WIL* B77 ....46 D3
Crutchley Av
POL/KGSB/FAZ B78 ....45 F2
Cuckoo Cl *HEDN* WS12 ....16 A4
Cumberland Crs *BNTWD* WS7 ....28 C1
Cumberland Dr
POL/KGSB/FAZ B78 ....45 F3
Cumberland Rd *CNCK/NC* WS11 ....15 G2
Cumberledge Hl *RUGE* WS15 ....18 A1
Curborough Rd *LICH* WS13 ....21 H3
Curlew *TAM/AM/WIL* B77 ....46 D5
Curlew Cl *LICHS* WS14 ....3 K5
Curlew Hl *CNCK/NC* WS11 ....15 G3
Curzon Pl *RUGE* WS15 ....9 E1
Cygnet Cl *HEDN* WS12 ....12 A4
Cypress Ri *HEDN* WS12 ....13 E5

D

Dace *TAM/AM/WIL* B77 ....46 A5
Daffodil Wk *RUGE* WS15 ....6 C4
Daintry Dr *POL/KGSB/FAZ* B78 ....40 A2
Daisy Bank *HEDN* WS12 ....11 F3
Dale Dr *BNTWD* WS7 ....28 D2
Dama Rd *POL/KGSB/FAZ* B78 ....45 E4
Dam St *LICH* WS13 ....2 C3
Danby Dr *HEDN* WS12 ....17 G2
Danelagh Cl *CRTAM* B79 ....41 E2
Danilo Rd *CNCK/NC* WS11 ....14 D5
Darges La *GTWY* WS6 ....25 F5
Dark La *GTWY* WS6 ....36 A3
LICH WS13 ....20 A5
POL/KGSB/FAZ B78 ....47 H4
Darnford La *LICHS* WS14 ....3 K6
Darnford Moors *LICHS* WS14 ....3 K7
Darnford Vw *LICH* WS13 ....3 J1
Dart *TAM/AM/WIL* B77 ....50 D2
Dartmouth Av *CNCK/NC* WS11 ....24 C1
Dartmouth Cl *CNCK/NC* WS11 ....24 C1
Dartmouth Rd *CNCK/NC* WS11 ....14 D5
Darwin Cl *BNTWD* WS7 ....28 D2
HEDN WS12 ....16 C5
LICH WS13 ....2 B1
Datteln Rd *CNCK/NC* WS11 ....15 G2
Davidson Rd *LICHS* WS14 ....2 D5
Davis Rd *TAM/AM/WIL* B77 ....42 C5
Davy Pl *RUGE* WS15 ....8 D2
Dayton Dr *RUGE* WS15 ....6 C3
Daywell Ri *RUGE* WS15 ....6 C2
Deacon Wy *RUGE* WS15 ....7 F3
Deakin Av *BRWNH* WS8 ....38 B3
Deal Av *BNTWD* WS7 ....28 C1
Deanery Cl *RUGE* WS15 ....7 E3
Deans Cft *LICH* WS13 ....2 E4
Deans Slade Dr *LICHS* WS14 ....31 G5
Deavall Wy *CNCK/NC* WS11 ....15 H4
Dee Gv *CNCK/NC* WS11 ....24 D1
Deeley *TAM/AM/WIL* B77 ....46 D3
Deepdale *POL/KGSB/FAZ* B78 ....47 G3
Deer Cl *CNCK/NC* WS11 ....27 E2
Deerfold Crs *BNTWD* WS7 ....28 D2
Deerhill *TAM/AM/WIL* B77 ....47 F3
Deerhurst Ri *HEDN* WS12 ....12 D5
Deerleap Wy *RUGE* WS15 ....6 C4
Deer Pk *HEDN* * WS12 ....13 F3
Deer Park Rd
POL/KGSB/FAZ B78 ....44 D3
Delafield Wy *RUGE* WS15 ....6 C3
The Dell *CRTAM* B79 ....4 E1
HEDN WS12 ....16 D2
LICH WS13 ....31 F2
Delta Wy *CNCK/NC* WS11 ....24 D3
Deltic *TAM/AM/WIL* B77 ....46 D3
Denbury Cl *HEDN* WS12 ....16 B5
Denmark Ri *HEDN* WS12 ....12 B4
Denmark Vls *LICH* * WS13 ....30 C4
Dennis *TAM/AM/WIL* B77 ....46 B2
Dent St *CRTAM* B79 ....5 G3
Derwent *TAM/AM/WIL* B77 ....46 A3
Derwent Gv *BNTWD* WS7 ....29 F3
CNCK/NC WS11 ....24 D1
Devall Cl *RUGE* WS15 ....9 E1
Devon Rd *CNCK/NC* WS11 ....25 F1
Devonshire Dr
POL/KGSB/FAZ B78 ....45 F3
Dewsbury Dr *BNTWD* WS7 ....29 E3
Diamond Gv *HEDN* WS12 ....16 A4
Dimbles Hl *LICH* WS13 ....21 H5
Dimbles La *LICH* WS13 ....21 G4
Dodds La *LICH* WS13 ....19 E3
Dog La *TAM/AM/WIL* B77 ....43 E3
Don Gv *CNCK/NC* * WS11 ....24 D2
Dorado *TAM/AM/WIL* B77 ....50 A1
Dorchester Rd *CNCK/NC* WS11 ....14 B5
Dormer Av *TAM/AM/WIL* B77 ....5 K3
Dorset Cl *POL/KGSB/FAZ* B78 ....45 F3
Dorset Rd *HEDN* WS12 ....16 C5
Dosthill Rd (Two Gates)
TAM/AM/WIL B77 ....50 A1
Dove Cl *BNTWD* WS7 ....29 F3
Dovedale *CNCK/NC* WS11 ....15 G1
Dove Hollow *GTWY* WS6 ....35 F3
HEDN WS12 ....16 C2
Dovehouse Flds *LICHS* WS14 ....2 C7
Dovestone *POL/KGSB/FAZ* B78 ....47 G3
Downesway *CNCK/NC* WS11 ....14 C4
Downing Dr *CRTAM* B79 ....40 D4
Drake Cft *LICH* WS13 ....2 E2
Draycott Crs *TAM/AM/WIL* B77 ....45 H3
Drayton Manor Dr
POL/KGSB/FAZ B78 ....45 E5
Dryden Rd *CRTAM* B79 ....41 F2
Dual Wy *HEDN* WS12 ....10 C3
Dugdale Cl *HEDN* WS12 ....16 D3
Duke Rd *BNTWD* WS7 ....18 A5
Dumolo's La *TAM/AM/WIL* B77 ....46 B1
Dundalk La *GTWY* WS6 ....34 D3
Dunedin *TAM/AM/WIL* B77 ....46 D3
Dunstall La *POL/KGSB/FAZ* B78 ....4 B5
POL/KGSB/FAZ B78 ....40 B3
Dunster *TAM/AM/WIL* B77 ....45 H5
Dunston Cl *GTWY* WS6 ....35 E4
Dunston Dr *BNTWD* WS7 ....28 C1
Durham Cl *POL/KGSB/FAZ* B78 ....45 F2
Durham Dr *RUGE* WS15 ....8 D2
Durlston Cl *TAM/AM/WIL* B77 ....42 C4
Dursley Dr *CNCK/NC* WS11 ....14 B4
Dursley Rd *BNTWD* WS7 ....28 C2
Dyott Cl *LICH* WS13 ....23 E5

E

Eagle Cl *GTWY* WS6 ....34 D2
Eagle Dr *TAM/AM/WIL* B77 ....43 E5
Eagle Gv *HEDN* WS12 ....16 A5
Ealingham *TAM/AM/WIL* B77 ....47 E2
Earl Dr *BNTWD* WS7 ....18 A5
East Butts Rd *RUGE* WS15 ....6 B4
East Cannock Rd *HEDN* WS12 ....16 A2
Eastcote Crs *BNTWD* WS7 ....28 B4
Eastern Av *LICH* WS13 ....21 F4
Eastern Wy *CNCK/NC* WS11 ....15 G3
CNCK/NC WS11 ....25 F3
Eastgate *HEDN* WS12 ....17 E1
Eastgate St *BNTWD* WS7 ....28 A1
East St *CNCK/NC* WS11 ....25 E3
East Vw *TAM/AM/WIL* B77 ....46 B1
Eastwood Av *BNTWD* WS7 ....28 C1
Ebenezer St *HEDN* WS12 ....11 G4
Edale *TAM/AM/WIL* B77 ....47 E3
Eddenswood Cl
POL/KGSB/FAZ B78 ....48 D2
Eden Cl *HEDN* WS12 ....16 C4
Edgar Cl *CRTAM* B79 ....41 E2
Edge Hl *POL/KGSB/FAZ* B78 ....51 E5
Edgemoor Meadow
HEDN WS12 ....16 A5
Edison Cl *HEDN* WS12 ....12 A4
Edmonton Cl *CNCK/NC* WS11 ....15 H4
Edwards Cl *RUGE* * WS15 ....7 E4
Edwards Rd *BNTWD* WS7 ....28 B4
Edward St *CNCK/NC* WS11 ....15 E2
CRTAM B79 ....4 D3
Elder Cl *CNCK/NC* WS11 ....16 A4
Elder La *BNTWD* WS7 ....29 E2
Elgar Cl *CNCK/NC* WS11 ....15 E1
LICH WS13 ....21 H4
Elias Cl *LICHS* WS14 ....3 J7
Eliot Cl *CRTAM* B79 ....41 F2
Elizabeth Dr *CRTAM* B79 ....41 F2
Elizabeth Rd *CNCK/NC* WS11 ....11 E5
Ellerbeck *TAM/AM/WIL* B77 ....47 E3
Ellesmere Rd *CNCK/NC* WS11 ....24 B1
Elliott Cl *CNCK/NC* WS11 ....15 F1
Ellis Wk *CNCK/NC* WS11 ....25 F1
Elm Gdns *LICHS* WS14 ....2 E5
Elm Gv *HEDN* WS12 ....10 D3
Elmhurst Dr *BNTWD* WS7 ....28 C5
Elmore La *RUGE* WS15 ....7 E4
Elm Rd *CNCK/NC* WS11 ....27 F4
Elms Dr *CNCK/NC* WS11 ....14 C5
Elmwood Cl *CNCK/NC* WS11 ....15 G3
Elunda Gv *BNTWD* WS7 ....28 A3
Ely Cl *CNCK/NC* WS11 ....15 H5
Emberton Wy *TAM/AM/WIL* B77 ....42 C4
Emmanuel Rd *BNTWD* WS7 ....28 D2
Engine La *BRWNH* WS8 ....37 G4
TAM/AM/WIL B77 ....46 D2
Ennerdale Cl *BRWNH* WS8 ....38 A5
Epsom Cl *LICHS* WS14 ....3 H4
TAM/AM/WIL B77 ....49 H4
Erasmus Wy *LICH* WS13 ....2 A2
Eringden *TAM/AM/WIL* B77 ....47 E3
Eskrett St *HEDN* WS12 ....15 H1
Essex Dr *HEDN* WS12 ....15 H2
RUGE WS15 ....8 D2
Essington Cl *LICHS* WS14 ....31 G4
Estridge La *GTWY* WS6 ....35 G2
Etchell Rd *POL/KGSB/FAZ* B78 ....4 B6
Etching Hill Rd *RUGE* WS15 ....6 A4
Ethelfleda Rd *TAM/AM/WIL* B77 ....50 C2
Europa Wy *LICHS* WS14 ....32 D1
Evans Cft *POL/KGSB/FAZ* B78 ....45 F3
Everglade Rd
POL/KGSB/FAZ B78 ....51 E5
Evergreen Hts *HEDN* WS12 ....11 G3
Exeter Dr *CRTAM* B79 ....40 D4
Exeter Rd *CNCK/NC* WS11 ....24 B1
Exley *TAM/AM/WIL* B77 ....46 A3

F

Fairfield Cl *HEDN* WS12 ....16 B5
Fairford Gdns *BNTWD* WS7 ....29 E3
Fair Lady Dr *BNTWD* WS7 ....27 H1
Fairmount Dr *CNCK/NC* WS11 ....25 E1
Fairmount Wy *RUGE* WS15 ....6 C4
Fair Oaks Dr *GTWY* WS6 ....35 G4
Fairview Cl *GTWY* WS6 ....34 D2
TAM/AM/WIL B77 ....42 C4
Fairway *CNCK/NC* WS11 ....24 D3
TAM/AM/WIL B77 ....50 B2
Falcon *TAM/AM/WIL* B77 ....50 D1
Falcon Cl *CNCK/NC* WS11 ....14 C4
GTWY WS6 ....34 C2
Fallow Fld *CNCK/NC* WS11 ....15 E3
LICH WS13 ....21 H3
Fallow Pk *HEDN* * WS12 ....12 B3
Falmouth Dr *TAM/AM/WIL* B77 ....42 C4
Falna Crs *CRTAM* B79 ....41 E2
Farewell La *BNTWD* WS7 ....29 G3
Faringdon *TAM/AM/WIL* B77 ....46 C3
Farm Cl *CRTAM* B79 ....41 H2
HEDN WS12 ....16 A3
RUGE WS15 ....6 C3
Fasson Cl *TAM/AM/WIL* B77 ....45 H4
Fazeley Rd *POL/KGSB/FAZ* B78 ....4 D5
POL/KGSB/FAZ B78 ....45 G2
Featherbed La *LICH* WS13 ....21 E3
Fecknam Wy *LICH* WS13 ....22 A4
Felspar Rd *TAM/AM/WIL* B77 ....46 D1
Felstead Cl *TAM/AM/WIL* B77 ....49 H3
Fennel Cl *GTWY* WS6 ....34 D1
Fenn St *TAM/AM/WIL* B77 ....46 A3

Ferncombe Dr *RUGE* WS15 ....6 C3
Fern Cft *LICH* WS13 ....21 F5
Ferndale Cl *BNTWD* WS7............28 C3
Ferndale Rd *LICH* WS13............21 F4
Fern Dell Cl *CNCK/NC* WS11 ......14 C4
Fern Dr *GTWY* WS6............25 G5
Fernleigh Av *BNTWD* WS7 ......28 C1
Fern Rd *HEDN* WS12............14 D1
Fernwood Dr *RUGE* WS15............6 D3
Ferrers Rd *TAM/AM/WIL* B77 ......5 K4
Ferrie Gv *BRWNH* WS8............38 A4
Festival Ct *CNCK/NC* * WS11......15 E1
Festival Ms *HEDN* WS12............11 F5
Fieldfare *BNTWD* WS7............29 F4
Field Farm Rd *TAM/AM/WIL* B77...46 A2
Fieldhouse Rd *BNTWD* WS7 ......28 C2
 HEDN WS12............11 F4
Field La *GTWY* WS6............35 F1
Field Pl *RUGE* WS15............8 B1
Field Rd *LICH* WS13............21 H3
Field St *CNCK/NC* WS11............15 F3
Filey *TAM/AM/WIL* B77............42 C4
Filey Cl *CNCK/NC* WS11............24 C1
Filton Av *BNTWD* WS7............28 C1
Finches Hl *RUGE* WS15............6 C5
Fir Cl *HEDN* WS12............10 D3
Fircroft Cl *CNCK/NC* WS11......15 C3
Firecrest Cl *HEDN* WS12......16 A4
First Av *BRWNH* WS8............38 C4
The Firs *RUGE* WS15............18 B1
Fir Tree Cl *CRTAM* B79 ......40 D2
Fisher St *HEDN* WS12............11 F3
Fives Gv *BNTWD* WS7............27 C1
Flaxley Rd *RUGE* WS15............8 D2
Flinn Cl *LICHS* WS14............3 H5
Flora Cl *CRTAM* B79 ......41 H2
Florence St *HEDN* WS12......11 G4
Florendine St *TAM/AM/WIL* B77 ...42 C4
Fontenaye Rd *CRTAM* B79......40 D2
Ford La *LICH* WS13............20 A4
Forest Gld *GTWY* * WS6............35 F2
Forest Wy *GTWY* WS6............35 G3
The Forge *CRTAM* B79......29 F4
Forge Cl *BNTWD* WS7............29 F4
Forge La *BNTWD* WS7............29 H3
 LICH WS13............2 A1
Forge Rd *RUGE* WS15............7 F4
Forge St *HEDN* WS12............16 A2
Forrest Av *CNCK/NC* WS11 ......25 E2
Fortescue La *RUGE* WS15............7 E3
Forties *TAM/AM/WIL* B77......46 B5
Fossdale Rd *TAM/AM/WIL* B77 ...46 D4
Fosseway *LICH* WS14............31 G4
Fosseway La *LICH* WS13............30 D5
Foster Av *HEDN* WS12............11 F5
Fourth Av *BRWNH* WS8............38 C3
Foxcroft Cl *BNTWD* WS7............28 D3
Foxes Rake *CNCK/NC* WS11 ......15 E3
Foxfields Wy *HEDN* WS12......10 C4
Foxglove *TAM/AM/WIL* B77 ......42 D5
Foxglove Cl *LICHS* WS14 ......31 G4
 RUGE WS15............6 C4
Foxhill Cl *HEDN* WS12............16 B4
Foxhill's Cl *BNTWD* WS7............28 C4
Foxland Av *GTWY* WS6............35 G1
Fox La *LICH* WS13............21 G2
Francis Rd *LICH* WS13............21 G4
Frank Gee Cl *RUGE* WS15............6 A4
Franklin Dr *BNTWD* WS7............28 D3
Frank Rogers Wk *RUGE* WS15......6 D3
Frederick Ct *TAM/AM/WIL* B77 ...46 B1
Freeford Gdns *LICHS* WS14 ......3 K6
Freer Dr *BNTWD* WS7............29 C2
Freeth Rd *BRWNH* WS8............38 C3
Fremantle Dr *HEDN* WS12......16 C4
French Av *POL/KGSB/FAZ* B78...44 B3
Frensham Cl *GTWY* WS6............25 E5
Freville Cl *CRTAM* B79............4 C1
Friars Wk *TAM/AM/WIL* B77......5 H6
The Friary *LICH* WS13............2 B5
Friary Av *LICH* WS13............2 B5
Friary Gdns *LICH* WS13............2 A5
Friary Rd *LICH* WS13............2 A5
Friary Vw *LICH* WS13............2 A4
Friday Acre *LICH* WS13............21 G5
Frobisher Cl *GTWY* WS6............35 F3
Frog La *LICH* WS13............2 B5
Furness *TAM/AM/WIL* B77............5 K7
Furst St *BRWNH* WS8............38 C4

G

Gable Cft *LICHS* WS14............3 K6
Gaelic Rd *CNCK/NC* WS11 ......14 D2
Gagarin *CRTAM* B79............4 A2
Gaiafields Rd *LICH* WS13............2 C1

Gaialands Crs *LICH* WS13 ....2 C1
Gaia La *LICH* WS13............2 C2
Gaiastowe *LICH* WS13............2 D1
Gainsborough Dr
 POL/KGSB/FAZ B78............44 A4
Gainsbrook Crs *CNCK/NC* WS11...26 D4
Gains La *BLOX/PEL* WS3............36 B2
Galena Cl *TAM/AM/WIL* B77......47 E2
Galliers Cl *TAM/AM/WIL* B77......50 C2
Galway Rd *BNTWD* WS7............28 C1
Garage Cl *TAM/AM/WIL* B77......5 K2
Garden Dr *RUGE* WS15............6 D4
Garden Vw *RUGE* WS15............6 D4
Garrick Ri *BNTWD* WS7............28 D2
 RUGE WS15............9 H2
Garrick Rd *CNCK/NC* WS11 ......14 D2
 LICH WS13............21 F4
Garrigill *TAM/AM/WIL* B77 ......46 D3
The Garth *LICH* WS13............21 H4
Gawsworth *CRTAM* B79 ......40 C2
Gayle *TAM/AM/WIL* B77......46 D3
Gemini Dr *CNCK/NC* WS11............25 F1
George Av *POL/KGSB/FAZ* B78...44 B3
George Brealey Cl *RUGE* WS15 ...9 F1
George La *LICH* WS13............2 E3
George St *HEDN* WS12............16 A2
Georgian Pl *CNCK/NC* WS11......15 E4
Gerard *CRTAM* B79............40 D2
Giffords Cft *LICH* WS13............21 G5
Gilbert Rd *LICH* WS13............22 A4
Giles Rd *LICH* WS13............21 G3
Gillway *CRTAM* B79 ....41 G1
Gilpins Cft *GTWY* WS6............34 D3
Girton Rd *CNCK/NC* WS11......25 F1
The Glade *LICH* WS13............14 C4
Gladstone Rd *HEDN* WS12......16 C5
Glascote La *TAM/AM/WIL* B77 ...46 C5
Glascote Rd *TAM/AM/WIL* B77......5 H5
 TAM/AM/WIL B77............47 H2
Glasscroft Cottages
 BNTWD WS7............29 H2
Gledhill Pk *LICHS* WS14............32 A4
Glen Cl *HEDN* WS12............14 D1
Glencoe Dr *CNCK/NC* WS11...15 G2
Glendale Ct *TAM/AM/WIL* B77......51 E1
Glendale Gdns *CNCK/NC* WS11...15 G2
Glendawn Cl *CNCK/NC* WS11 ......15 G3
Glendene Rd *HEDN* WS12......12 A5
Gleneagles *TAM/AM/WIL* B77 ......43 E4
Glenhaven *RUGE* WS15............6 C3
Glenmore Av *BNTWD* WS7............28 C3
Glenthorne Dr *GTWY* WS6......35 E1
Gloucester Cl *LICH* WS13............21 H5
Gloucester Wy *CNCK/NC* WS11 ...15 H5
Glovers Cl *HEDN* WS12............17 E1
Glover St *HEDN* WS12............16 D3
Glyndebourne *CRTAM* B79............40 C2
Godolphin *CRTAM* B79 ....40 C3
Gofton *TAM/AM/WIL* B77......46 D1
Goldcrest *TAM/AM/WIL* B77......50 D1
Goldsborough
 TAM/AM/WIL B77............46 D3
Goldsmith Pl *CRTAM* B79......41 F2
Goldthorne Av *CNCK/NC* WS7......5 K4
Goodwood Cl *HEDN* * WS12......17 E1
 LICHS WS14............14 D4
Goostry Cl *TAM/AM/WIL* B77 ......5 K4
Goostry Rd *TAM/AM/WIL* B77 ......5 K3
Gorseburn Wy *RUGE* WS15............6 A4
Gorse Dr *HEDN* WS12............14 D1
Gorse La *LICHS* WS14............3 H7
 RUGE WS15............6 C3
Gorsemoor Rd *HEDN* WS12......16 B5
Gorse Rd *RUGE* WS15............9 F2
Gorseway *BNTWD* WS7............28 D4
Gorsey La *BLOX/PEL* WS3............36 D3
 CNCK/NC WS11............14 B5
Gorstey Lea *BNTWD* WS7......29 E2
Gorsty Bank *LICHS* WS14............3 J3
Gorsy Bank Rd
 TAM/AM/WIL B77............50 C2
Gowland Dr *CNCK/NC* WS11......14 B5
Goya Cl *HEDN* WS12............16 A4
Grainger Ct *CNCK/NC* * WS11 ......14 D4
Granary Cl *HEDN* WS12............15 H1
Grange Av *TAM/AM/WIL* B77......15 F4
Grange Ct *TAM/AM/WIL* B77......45 H4
Grange La *LICH* WS13............21 E3
 LICH WS13............30 C3
Grange Rd *BNTWD* WS7............28 C4
 CNCK/NC WS11............27 F3
Granville *TAM/AM/WIL* B77......46 C5
Grasmere Pl *CNCK/NC* WS11......15 E1
Grassholme *TAM/AM/WIL* B77...46 D4
Grasmere Ct *GTWY* WS6......30 D1
Gratley Cft *HEDN* WS12............14 C2

Gravel La *HEDN* WS12............10 B5
Grayling *TAM/AM/WIL* B77......50 A1
Gray Rd *HEDN* WS12............11 F5
Grayston Av *TAM/AM/WIL* B77 ...42 B5
Great Charles St *BRWNH* WS8 ...38 B4
Greatmead *TAM/AM/WIL* B77 ......45 H3
Greenacre Cl *TAM/AM/WIL* B77 ...43 E4
Greenacres *RUGE* WS15............8 D1
Greencroft *LICH* WS13............21 G4
Greenfields *CNCK/NC* WS11 ......15 G4
Greenfields Dr *RUGE* WS15............6 D4
Greenheart *TAM/AM/WIL* B77 ...42 D5
Green Heath Rd *HEDN* WS12......11 G3
Greenhill Cl *TAM/AM/WIL* B77 ......49 H2
Greenhill Ms *LICH* WS13............2 E3
Greenhough Rd *LICH* WS13............2 A2
The Green *CNCK/NC* WS11............14 D5
 POL/KGSB/FAZ B78............44 D2
 POL/KGSB/FAZ B78............51 E3
 RUGE WS15............6 D3
 TAM/AM/WIL B77............43 E4
Green La *BNTWD* WS7............19 F5
 BNTWD WS7............38 D2
 CNCK/NC WS11............25 E3
 LICH WS13............19 E3
 POL/KGSB/FAZ B78............47 F5
 RUGE WS15............6 D3
Green Lea *TAM/AM/WIL* B77 ......46 D4
Green Mdw *HEDN* WS12............16 A5
Green Slade Gv *HEDN* WS12......12 A4
Greenwood Dr *LICHS* WS14 ....2 D6
Greenwood Pk *HEDN* WS12......11 H5
Gregory Rd *BNTWD* WS7............29 C2
Greig Ct *CNCK/NC* WS11............16 A4
Gresham Rd *CNCK/NC* WS11 ......15 E3
Gresley *TAM/AM/WIL* B77......46 C3
Gresley Rw *LICH* WS13............2 E3
Greyfriars Dr *CRTAM* B79......40 D4
Griffin Cl *BNTWD* WS7............28 A1
Grimley Wy *CNCK/NC* WS11......15 F2
Grindcobbe Gv *RUGE* WS15......6 D3
Grindsbrook *TAM/AM/WIL* B77 ...46 D4
Grosvenor Cl *LICHS* WS14............3 G7
The Grove *BNTWD* WS7............27 H1
Grove Cl *CNCK/NC* WS11......26 D4
Grove La *BLOX/PEL* WS3............36 C3
Gullick Wy *BNTWD* WS7............27 H1
Gurnard *TAM/AM/WIL* B77......50 A1
Guys Cl *CRTAM* B79............41 E2

H

Hadrians Cl *TAM/AM/WIL* B77 ......46 A4
Hagley Dr *RUGE* WS15............6 D4
Hagley Park Gdns *RUGE* WS15 ...8 D1
Hagley Rd *RUGE* WS15............6 D4
Haig Cl *CNCK/NC* WS11............15 G1
Halford St *CRTAM* B79............4 C3
Hallcourt Cl *CNCK/NC* * WS11......25 E1
Hallcourt Crs *CNCK/NC* WS11......25 E1
Hallcourt La *CNCK/NC* WS11......25 E1
Hall La *BNTWD* WS7............29 G5
 GTWY WS6............25 F5
Hall Meadow *TAM/AM/WIL* B77......24 B3
Halston Rd *BNTWD* WS7............28 D2
Haltonlea *TAM/AM/WIL* B77......46 D4
Hamble *TAM/AM/WIL* B77 ......46 A2
Hamelin St *CNCK/NC* WS11......15 E3
Hamilton Cl *HEDN* WS12............16 D1
Hamilton Lea *CNCK/NC* WS11......27 E3
The Hamlet *CNCK/NC* WS11......26 C4
Hammerwich La *BNTWD* WS7......39 H1
Hammerwich Rd *BNTWD* WS7......29 F3
Hamps Cl *BNTWD* WS7............29 F2
Hampshire Cl
 POL/KGSB/FAZ B78............45 E2
Hampton Cl *CRTAM* B79............41 H2
Hampton Gn *CNCK/NC* WS11......24 D2
Hampton St *CNCK/NC* WS11......24 D2
Hanbury Rd *BRWNH* WS8............38 A2
 CNCK/NC WS11............26 D4
 TAM/AM/WIL B77............42 C5
Handel Ct *CNCK/NC* WS11......16 A4
Hanlith *TAM/AM/WIL* B77......46 D4
Hannaford Wy *CNCK/NC* WS11 ...15 F4
Hanney Hay Rd *BNTWD* WS7......38 D1
Hanover Pl *CNCK/NC* WS11......15 E4
Hardie Av *RUGE* WS15............9 E1
Hardie Gn *CNCK/NC* WS11......15 F3
Hardwick Ct *CRTAM* B79............5 G3
Harebell *TAM/AM/WIL* B77......42 D5
Harebell Cl *HEDN* WS12............16 B4
Harley Cl *RUGE* WS15............9 F2
Harney Ct *RUGE* WS15............6 D2
Harrison Cl *GTWY* WS6............34 D3
Harrison Rd *CNCK/NC* WS11......25 E2

Hartlebury Cl *HEDN* WS12............
Hartleyburn *TAM/AM/WIL* B77
Hartslade *LICHS* WS14............
Hartwell La *GTWY* WS6............
Harwell Cl *CRTAM* B79............
Harwood Dr *TAM/AM/WIL* B77
Harwood Rd *LICH* WS13............
Hastings Cl *TAM/AM/WIL* B77
Hatherton Cft *CNCK/NC* WS11
Hatherton Rd *CNCK/NC* WS11
Hatherton St *GTWY* WS6............
Hatton Rd *CNCK/NC* WS11............
Havefield Av *LICHS* WS14............
Hawfinch *TAM/AM/WIL* B77............
Hawkesmoor Dr *LICHS* WS14..
Hawkins Cl *LICH* WS13............
Hawkins Dr *CNCK/NC* WS11 ......
Hawks Cl *GTWY* WS6............
Hawks Green La *CNCK/NC* WS1
Hawkside *TAM/AM/WIL* B77 ..
Hawksworth *TAM/AM/WIL* B77
Hawkyard Ct *CNCK/NC* WS11
Hawthorn Av *GTWY* WS6............
Hawthorn Cl *LICH* WS13............
Hawthorne Av *CRTAM* B79..
Hawthorne Crs *BNTWD* WS7..
Hawthorne Rd *GTWY* WS6............
 HEDN WS12............
 HEDN WS12............
Hawthorn Wy *RUGE* WS15............
Hayes Vw *LICH* WS13............
Hayes View Dr *GTWY* WS6............
Hayes Wy *CNCK/NC* WS11............
Hayfield Hl *RUGE* WS15............
Hayle *TAM/AM/WIL* B77 ....
Haymoor *LICHS* WS14............
Hayworth Cl *CRTAM* B79 ......
Hayworth Rd *LICH* WS13............
Hazel Dr *HEDN* WS12............
Hazelgarth *TAM/AM/WIL* B77 .
Hazel Gv *LICHS* WS14............
Hazel La *GTWY* WS6............
Hazelmere Dr *BNTWD* WS7......
Hazelwood Cl *GTWY* WS6............
Hazlemere Gv *CNCK/NC* WS11..
Healey *TAM/AM/WIL* B77............
Heart of England Wy *LICH* WS5
 POL/KGSB/FAZ B78............
Heathbank Dr *HEDN* WS12............
Heather Cl *RUGE* WS15............
Heather Dr *HEDN* WS12............
Heather Ms *HEDN* WS12............
Heather Rd *HEDN* WS12............
Heather Va *HEDN* WS12............
Heath Gap Rd *CNCK/NC* WS11 .
Heathland Cl *HEDN* WS12............
Heathley La *POL/KGSB/FAZ* B7
Heath Rd *RUGE* * WS15............
Heath St *CRTAM* B79 ....
 HEDN WS12............
Heath Vw *BNTWD* WS7............
 HEDN * WS12............
Heath Wy *CNCK/NC* WS11............
Hebden *TAM/AM/WIL* B77 ....
Hedgerow Cl *HEDN* WS12............
The Hedgerows
 TAM/AM/WIL B77............
Hedging La *TAM/AM/WIL* B77..
Hednesford Rd *BRWNH* WS8 ...
 CNCK/NC WS11............
 CNCK/NC WS11............
 HEDN WS12............
 RUGE WS15............
Hednesford St *CNCK/NC* WS11
Heenan Gv *LICH* WS13............
Heligan Pl *HEDN* * WS12............
Helmingham *CRTAM* B79..
Helston Cl *CRTAM* B79............
Hemlock Wy *CNCK/NC* WS11 ..
Henderson Cl *LICHS* WS14......
Henley Cl *BNTWD* WS7............
 CRTAM B79............
Henley Gra *RUGE* WS15............
Hereford Rd *HEDN* WS12............
Hereford Wy
 POL/KGSB/FAZ B78............
Heritage Ct *LICHS* WS14 ......
Hermes Rd *LICH* WS13............
Hermitage La
 POL/KGSB/FAZ B78............
Herondale *HEDN* WS12............
Heron St *RUGE* WS15............
Hesleden *TAM/AM/WIL* B77......
Hewitt Cl *LICH* WS13............
Hewston Cft *HEDN* WS12............
Hickory Cl *CNCK/NC* * WS11......
High Bank *CNCK/NC* WS11......

...me Ct
.B/FAZ B78 ....4 D6
Rd TAM/AM/WIL B77 ....46 A4
Crs LICHS WS14 ....2 E5
AV BNTWD WS7 ....28 D2
/WIL B77 ....42 D4
Cl BNTWD WS7 ....28 D2
Gdns LICHS WS14 ....3 J6
d BNTWD WS7 ....28 D2
512 ....16 C5
BNTWD WS7 ....28 D2
Gra GTWY WS6 ....34 D3
Pk GTWY WS6 ....34 D3
Rd BNTWD WS7 ....28 B5
CH WS13 ....21 F5
VCK/NC WS11 ....14 D5
n Ct CNCK/NC * WS11 ..14 D5
Cl CRTAM B79 ....41 G2
d HEDN WS12 ....14 C2
 ....6 C2
low RUGE WS15 ....18 B1
nt St HEDN WS12 ....11 H5
WS15 ....6 C1
TWD WS7 ....18 A5
WS8 ....38 B5
WS11 ....27 F4
56 ....34 C2
/WIL B77 ....49 H3
st RUGE WS15 ....9 E2
CRTAM B79 ....41 G3
r LICH WS13 ....2 A1
i BNTWD WS7 ....28 D5
CK/NC WS11 ....15 C3
M/AM/WIL B77 ....46 B2
HS WS14 ....3 G7
BNTWD WS7 ....28 A4
512 ....11 G4
15 ....9 H3
WD WS7 ....28 A4
WS11 ....26 D3
56 ....34 C2
512 ....16 A3
515 ....7 E5
GE WS15 ....18 B1
CRTAM B79 ....41 G1
56 ....6 C4
Vy TAM/AM/WIL B77 ..46 B4
GTWY WS6 ....35 G2
BNTWD WS7 ....27 G1
POL/KGSB/FAZ B78 ....44 A2
RUGE WS15 ....19 E1
HEDN WS12 ....16 C4
RUGE WS15 ....9 H3
ICH WS13 ....3 J1
Hill La BNTWD WS7 ....19 C5
TAM/AM/WIL B77 ....46 C5
TAM/AM/WIL B77 ....43 E3
CNCK/NC WS11 ....15 H4
LICH WS13 ....23 E5
CNCK/NC WS11 ....15 F5
CRTAM B79 ....4 E4
rk Rd CNCK/NC WS11 ..9 E1
e La BNTWD WS7 ....18 A5
Rd RUGE WS15 ....18 A1
TWY WS6 ....35 F4
512 ....16 C4
VCK/NC WS11 ....11 F5
HEDN WS12 ....16 A5
Cl TAM/AM/WIL B77 ..46 A3
CK/NC WS11 ....15 H4
AM/AM/WIL B77 ....47 E4
Pl RUGE WS15 ....6 C2
RI LICHS WS13 ....3 C6
BRWNH WS8 ....37 H5
urne TAM/AM/WIL B77 ..46 C5
kle Wy GTWY WS6 ......25 H5
TAM/AM/WIL B77 ....42 A5
eadow HEDN WS12 ....16 A5
n TAM/AM/WIL B77 ....42 D5
n Crs HEDN WS12 ......13 C5
RUGE WS15 ....8 B1
RUGE WS15 ....7 E5
e Dr RUGE * WS15 ......6 B4
a GTWY WS6 ....34 B2
d BNTWD WS7 ....28 D5
t CRTAM B79 ....41 E1
AM/AM/WIL B77 ....46 B4
rs HEDN WS12 ....12 A4
a BRWNH WS8 ....38 B2
AM/AM/WIL B77 ....43 E5
ord La LICH WS13 ....33 G2
CNCK/NC WS11 ....15 H4

Hudson Dr BNTWD WS7 ....29 E3
Hunslet Rd BNTWD WS7 ....28 D1
Hunter Av BNTWD WS7 ....28 D2
Hunter Cl LICHS WS14 ....3 H7
Hunter Rd CNCK/NC WS11 ....25 E1
Huntingdon Cl
  POL/KGSB/FAZ B78 ....45 E2
Huntington Terrace Rd
  CNCK/NC WS11 ....15 F2
Huntsmans Ga BNTWD WS7 ....28 D1
Huntsmans Ri HEDN WS12 ....10 C3
Huntsmans Wk RUGE WS15 ....6 C4
Huron Cl CNCK/NC WS11 ....15 H4
Hurstbourne Cl RUGE WS15 ....6 C3
Hussey Rd BRWNH WS8 ....38 A4
  CNCK/NC WS11 ....26 D4
Hutchinson Cl RUGE WS15 ....6 B3
Hut Hill La GTWY WS6 ....25 G5
Hyssop Cl CNCK/NC WS11 ....15 H4

I

Ingestre Cl CNCK/NC WS11 ....15 H5
Ingleside RUGE * WS15 ....6 C4
Ingram Pit La TAM/AM/WIL B77 ....42 D4
Iris Cl CRTAM B79 ....41 H3
Ironstone Rd BNTWD WS7 ....28 A1
  HEDN WS12 ....17 G2
Irving Cl LICH WS13 ....21 E4
Irwell La TAM/AM/WIL B77 ....46 B2
Ivanhoe Rd LICH WS13 ....2 C6
Ivatt TAM/AM/WIL B77 ....46 C2
Ivy Cl CNCK/NC WS11 ....24 C1
Ivy La RUGE WS15 ....18 B1

J

Jackson Cl CNCK/NC WS11 ....26 C5
Jackson Rd LICH WS13 ....21 H3
Jacob's Hall La GTWY WS6 ....35 G3
Jade Gv HEDN WS12 ....16 A4
Jaguar TAM/AM/WIL B77 ....46 B2
James St CNCK/NC WS11 ....15 F1
James Warner Cl RUGE WS15 ....6 D4
Jasmine Rd TAM/AM/WIL B77 ....42 D5
Jason Cl TAM/AM/WIL B77 ....5 K2
Jeffery Cl RUGE WS15 ....5 F1
Jenkinstown Rd HEDN WS12 ....13 E5
Jensen TAM/AM/WIL B77 ....46 B2
Jerome Dr CNCK/NC WS11 ....27 E4
Jerome Rd CNCK/NC WS11 ....26 D4
Jerome Wy BNTWD WS7 ....28 D2
Jervis Rd TAM/AM/WIL B77 ....50 C2
Jesmond Dr HEDN WS12 ....17 E1
Jessop Dr TAM/AM/WIL B77 ....5 K3
Jockey HI LICHS * WS14 ....32 D4
John Ball Cl RUGE WS15 ....6 D4
Johndory TAM/AM/WIL B77 ....50 A1
Johns La GTWY WS6 ....35 F1
Johnson Cl LICH WS13 ....22 A5
  RUGE WS15 ....6 A3
Johnson Rd BNTWD WS7 ....28 B1
  CNCK/NC WS11 ....14 D2
John St CNCK/NC WS11 ....15 F1
  HEDN WS12 ....16 D3
  TAM/AM/WIL B77 ....46 B1
John Till Cl RUGE WS15 ....7 E4
Jones' La BNTWD WS7 ....29 H2
  GTWY WS6 ....35 H3
  RUGE WS15 ....6 C5
Jonkel Av TAM/AM/WIL B77 ....50 D3
Jordan Cl LICH WS13 ....2 A2
Joseph Dewsbury Cl
  BNTWD WS7 ....28 A1
Joseph Dix Dr RUGE WS15 ....6 D3
Jowett TAM/AM/WIL B77 ....46 A2
Jubilee Cl GTWY WS6 ....35 F3
Jubilee St RUGE WS15 ....6 D4
Julian Cl GTWY WS6 ....35 G1
June Crs TAM/AM/WIL B77 ....42 B4
Juniper TAM/AM/WIL B77 ....42 D5
Juniper Cl HEDN WS12 ....13 E5

K

Kean Cl LICH WS13 ....21 E4
Keats Av CNCK/NC WS11 ....15 E1
Keats Cl CRTAM B79 ....41 E1
Keble Cl BNTWD WS7 ....29 E2
  CNCK/NC WS11 ....25 E1
Keble Wk CRTAM B79 ....4 D1
Keeling Dr CNCK/NC WS11 ....14 B5

Keeper's Cl BNTWD WS7 ....28 C3
  LICHS WS14 ....3 J5
Kelly Av RUGE WS15 ....9 F2
Kelvedon Wy RUGE WS15 ....6 C4
Kelvin Dr CNCK/NC WS11 ....15 G3
Kempton Cl HEDN WS12 ....13 E5
Kempton Dr GTWY WS6 ....35 F2
Kendal Ct CNCK/NC WS11 ....24 B1
Kenilworth Dr CNCK/NC WS11 ......14 D2
Kenilworth Rd LICHS WS13 ....2 D6
  TAM/AM/WIL B77 ....42 B5
Kenmore Av HEDN WS12 ....11 F4
Kennedy Cl TAM/AM/WIL B77 ....45 H3
Kennet TAM/AM/WIL B77 ....46 A3
Kennet Cl BRWNH WS8 ....37 G2
Kensington Dr CRTAM B79 ....41 G2
Kent Av POL/KGSB/FAZ B78 ....45 F3
Kent Pl HEDN WS12 ....16 D5
Kentwell CRTAM B79 ....40 C2
Kepler CRTAM B79 ....40 D2
Kerria Rd TAM/AM/WIL B77 ....43 E5
Kestrel TAM/AM/WIL B77 ....50 D1
Kestrel Gv HEDN WS12 ....16 A5
Kestrel Wy GTWY WS6 ....34 C2
Kettlebrook Rd
  TAM/AM/WIL B77 ....5 H6
Keys Park Rd HEDN WS12 ....16 C5
Keystone Rd RUGE WS15 ....7 F2
Kielder Cl HEDN WS12 ....16 C4
Kilbye Cl TAM/AM/WIL B77 ....50 C2
Kilmorie Rd CNCK/NC WS11 ....14 C4
Kimberley Av TAM/AM/WIL B77 ....46 C5
Kimberley Wy RUGE WS15 ....9 F3
Kingfisher TAM/AM/WIL B77 ....50 D1
Kingfisher Dr HEDN WS12 ....16 A2
Kings Av HEDN WS12 ....16 A2
Kingsbury Link
  POL/KGSB/FAZ * B78 ....50 D5
Kings Cft HEDN WS12 ....16 C2
Kingsdown Rd BNTWD WS7 ....18 A5
King's Hill Rd LICHS WS14 ....2 E7
Kingsley Av HEDN WS12 ....12 A4
Kingsley Cl CRTAM B79 ....41 F3
Kingston Cl CRTAM B79 ....41 H2
King St BNTWD WS7 ....28 B4
  CRTAM B79 ....4 E4
  RUGE WS15 ....7 F5
Kingsway CNCK/NC WS11 ....15 G2
Kingswood Av CNCK/NC WS11 ......24 D2
Kingswood Dr CNCK/NC WS11 ......26 D4
  GTWY WS6 ....25 G5
Kinross Av HEDN WS12 ....11 F4
Kinsall Gn TAM/AM/WIL B77 ....51 F1
Kipling Ri CRTAM B79 ....41 E1
Kirkland Wy POL/KGSB/FAZ B78 ....44 A4
Kirkside Gv BRWNH WS8 ....38 B5
Kirtley TAM/AM/WIL B77 ....46 B2
Knaves Castle Av BRWNH WS8 ......38 B2
Knighton Rd HEDN WS12 ....16 C3
Knight Rd BNTWD WS7 ....18 A5
Knights Ct CNCK/NC WS11 ....27 E5
Knoll Cl BNTWD WS7 ....28 C4
Kurtus TAM/AM/WIL B77 ....50 A1

L

Laburnum Av CNCK/NC WS11 ....24 D2
  CRTAM B79 ....41 G1
Laburnum Cl CNCK/NC WS11 ....25 E2
Laburnum Gv BNTWD WS7 ....28 B3
Lady Bank CRTAM B79 ....4 E4
Lady Br POL/KGSB/FAZ B78 ....4 E4
Lagonda TAM/AM/WIL B77 ....5 K7
Lagrange CRTAM B79 ....40 D3
Lakeland Dr TAM/AM/WIL B77 ......46 D5
Lakenheath CRTAM B79 ....41 H2
Lakeside Dr CNCK/NC WS11 ....27 E4
Lambert Dr BNTWD WS7 ....28 C2
Lambourne Cl GTWY WS6 ....35 F1
  LICHS WS14 ....3 J3
Lamprey TAM/AM/WIL B77 ....50 A1
Lancaster Rd LICH WS13 ....23 G1
Lance Dr BNTWD WS7 ....18 A5
Lanchester Cl CRTAM B79 ....40 D4
Landor Crs RUGE WS15 ....9 E2
Landwood Gn GTWY WS6 ....35 E2
Landwood La GTWY WS6 ....34 D2
Lanehead Wk RUGE WS15 ....6 C3
Langdale Ct RUGE WS15 ....7 F2
Langdale Dr CNCK/NC WS11 ....24 B2
Langholm CRTAM B79 ....16 C4
Langtree Cl HEDN WS12 ....16 B5
Lanrick Gdns CRTAM B79 ....7 E3
Lansbury Dr CNCK/NC WS11 ....15 E2
Lansbury Rd RUGE WS15 ....9 E2

Lansdowne Crs
  TAM/AM/WIL B77 ....46 A3
Lansdowne Wy RUGE WS15 ....6 C3
Lapwing TAM/AM/WIL B77 ....50 D1
Lapwing Cl GTWY WS6 ....34 C3
Larch Cl LICHS WS14 ....3 K5
Larch Rd RUGE WS15 ....9 F2
Larchwood Dr CNCK/NC WS11 ......15 G2
Larkholme Cl RUGE WS15 ....6 A4
Larkspur TAM/AM/WIL B77 ....50 A3
Larkspur Av BNTWD WS7 ....28 C4
Launceston Cl TAM/AM/WIL B77 ....46 A2
The Laurels RUGE WS15 ....9 F1
Laurel Bank CRTAM B79 ....4 E1
Laurel Cl LICH WS13 ....3 G3
Laurel Dr BNTWD WS7 ....29 E2
  HEDN WS12 ....16 C2
Lavender Rd TAM/AM/WIL B77 ......42 B5
Lawford Av LICHS WS14 ....3 J4
Lawnoaks Cl BRWNH WS8 ....37 H2
Lawnswood Av BNTWD WS7 ....28 B5
Lawnswood Cl HEDN WS12 ....16 B5
Lawrence Ct CRTAM B79 ....41 F3
Leacroft La CNCK/NC WS11 ....25 F4
Leafdown Cl HEDN WS12 ....16 B2
Leafenden Av BNTWD WS7 ....28 C4
Lea Hall La RUGE WS15 ....9 H3
Lea La GTWY WS6 ....35 G2
Leam Dr BNTWD WS7 ....29 F2
Leamington Cl CNCK/NC WS11 ......24 C1
Leander Cl BNTWD WS7 ....18 A5
  GTWY WS6 ....35 F3
The Leasowe LICH WS13 ....21 G5
Leasowe Rd RUGE WS15 ....9 G5
Leathermill La RUGE WS15 ....7 F4
Lebanon Gv BNTWD WS7 ....28 B1
Leedham Av TAM/AM/WIL B77 ....5 J3
Lees Cl RUGE WS15 ....9 H3
Legion Cl CNCK/NC WS11 ....27 E3
Leigh Av BNTWD WS7 ....28 D2
Leighswood Cl CNCK/NC WS11 ......26 D4
Leomansley Cl LICH WS13 ....31 F2
Leomansley Rd LICH WS13 ....31 F2
Leomansley Vw LICH WS13 ....31 F2
The Levels RUGE WS15 ....9 F3
Leveson Av GTWY WS6 ....35 G2
Levett Rd TAM/AM/WIL B77 ....43 E4
Levetts Flds LICH WS13 ....2 E4
Levetts Hollow HEDN WS12 ....16 B3
Levetts Sq LICH WS13 ....2 D4
Lewis Cl LICHS WS14 ....3 K4
Leyfields LICH WS13 ....21 H4
Leyland Dr RUGE WS15 ....7 E3
Leyland Rd TAM/AM/WIL B77 ....46 B2
Liberty Rd TAM/AM/WIL B77 ....50 C2
Libra Cl CRTAM B79 ....41 E2
Lichen Cl HEDN WS12 ....14 C1
Lichfield Crs POL/KGSB/FAZ B78 ....40 A2
Lichfield Rd ALDR WS9 ....39 F5
  BNTWD WS7 ....29 F5
  BRWNH WS8 ....38 B4
  CNCK/NC WS11 ....25 F1
  CRTAM B79 ....4 A2
  POL/KGSB/FAZ B78 ....40 A2
Lichfield St CRTAM B79 ....4 C3
  POL/KGSB/FAZ B78 ....45 E3
  RUGE WS15 ....7 F5
Lilac Av CNCK/NC WS11 ....24 D2
Lilac Gv BNTWD WS7 ....28 B2
Lilac La GTWY WS6 ....35 F4
Lilac Rd CRTAM B79 ....41 F1
Lillington Cl LICH WS13 ....2 F3
Lime Gv BNTWD WS7 ....29 E3
  LICH WS13 ....3 H3
Lime La BLOX/PEL WS3 ....37 E3
Limepit La HEDN WS12 ....11 E5
Lime Rd HEDN WS12 ....10 D3
Lincoln Cl LICH WS13 ....22 A3
Lincoln Dr CNCK/NC WS11 ....25 F1
Linden Av BNTWD WS7 ....28 B1
Linden Cl TAM/AM/WIL B77 ....42 C5
Linden Vw HEDN WS12 ....15 H2
Lindera TAM/AM/WIL B77 ....42 D5
Lindisfarne TAM/AM/WIL B77 ....46 A2
Lingfield Cl GTWY WS6 ....35 F2
Lingfield Dr GTWY WS6 ....35 F2
Ling Rd HEDN WS12 ....14 C1
Linnet Cl HEDN WS12 ....10 D4
Lintly TAM/AM/WIL B77 ....47 E3
Linwood Dr HEDN WS12 ....11 F4
Lion's Den LICHS WS14 ....39 C4
Lion St RUGE WS15 ....7 E4
Little Barrow Wk LICH WS13 ....2 A1
Little Church La CRTAM B79 ....5 F3
Littlecote CRTAM B79 ....40 C3
Little Gra LICH WS13 ....21 F5
Little Orch RUGE WS15 ....7 E3

Little Pipe La *LICH* WS13 ....20 A5
Littleton Dr *HEDN* WS12 ....10 C4
Littleton Wy *BNTWD* WS7 ....17 H5
Littlewood La *GTWY* WS6 ....25 E5
Littlewood Rd *GTWY* WS6................25 E5
Littleworth HI *HEDN* WS12..............16 B2
Littleworth Rd *HEDN* WS12 ....16 B2
Litton *TAM/AM/WIL* B77 ....47 F3
Lloyd George Gv *CNCK/NC* WS11....16 A4
Lloyd St *CNCK/NC* WS11 ....14 D5
Lochsong Cl *TAM/AM/WIL* B77 ......50 A3
Lock Keepers Cl *CNCK/NC* WS11 ....26 D4
Lockside Vw *RUGE* WS15................7 F5
Lodge La *CNCK/NC* WS11 ....24 B5
  LICH WS13 ....19 F3
Lodge Rd *BNTWD* WS7 ....18 A5
  RUGE WS15..............9 G2
Lodge Vw *GTWY* WS6....................34 C1
Loftus Ct *BNTWD* WS7....................28 B4
Lomax Cl *LICH* WS13 ....2 D1
Lomax Rd *HEDN* WS12 ....11 H4
Lombard Gdns *LICH* * WS13 ....2 D3
Lombard St *LICH* WS13....................2 D3
Lombardy Gv *BNTWD* WS7..............28 B1
Lomita Crs *TAM/AM/WIL* B77........46 A4
Lomond Cl *CRTAM* B79....................41 E1
London Rd *LICHS* WS14..................32 A4
Longacres *HEDN* WS12....................16 D1
Long Bridge Rd *LICHS* WS14............32 A4
Long Cft *HEDN* WS12......................14 C2
Longfellow Pl *CNCK/NC* WS11 ....15 E2
Longfellow Rd *BNTWD* WS7............18 B5
Longfield Cl *TAM/AM/WIL* B77........42 B5
Longford Rd *CNCK/NC* WS11 ....24 C1
Longlands Dr *TAM/AM/WIL* B77 ......42 C5
Longleat *CRTAM* B79......................40 C2
Longstaff Av *HEDN* WS12................17 G2
Longstaff Cft *LICH* WS13 ....21 F4
Lord Cromwell Ct
  CNCK/NC * WS11 ....15 C1
Lorne St *BNTWD* WS7 ....28 A1
Lorton *CRTAM* B79..........................40 C2
Lothersdale *TAM/AM/WIL* B77........47 E4
Lotus *TAM/AM/WIL* B77 ....46 B1
Lotus Dr *CNCK/NC* WS11 ....15 E1
Loughshaw *TAM/AM/WIL* B77 ....47 F3
Lovatt Pl *CNCK/NC* WS11 ....15 E1
Lovatt St *CNCK/NC* WS11 ....15 E1
Love La *GTWY* WS6........................35 C1
  RUGE WS15..............7 F4
Lovell *CRTAM* B79............................4 B1
Lovett Ct *RUGE* WS15......................6 D3
Lowdham *TAM/AM/WIL* B77 ....47 F3
Lower Brook St *RUGE* WS15..............7 E5
Lower Gungate *CRTAM* B79..............5 F2
Lower La *LICH* WS13 ....19 E4
Lowerpark *TAM/AM/WIL* B77 ....45 H3
Lower Rd *HEDN* WS12....................16 A3
Lower Sandford St *LICH* WS13 ....2 A4
Lowforce *TAM/AM/WIL* B77 ....47 F3
Lowland Rd *BNTWD* WS7................14 C1
Low St *GTWY* WS6 ....34 C1
Ludgate *CRTAM* B79 ....4 D2
Lud La *CRTAM* B79 ....4 D2
Ludlow Cl *HEDN* WS12....................16 A4
Lulworth Rd *BNTWD* WS7................28 C2
Lunns Cft *LICH* WS13........................2 E1
Lymington Rd *BNTWD* WS7..............18 B5
Lyn Av *LICH* WS13 ....21 F5
Lyndale *TAM/AM/WIL* B77 ....50 C1
Lyndhurst Rd *HEDN* WS12..............16 B5
Lyneham *CRTAM* B79......................41 C1
Lynfield Rd *LICH* WS13 ....21 F5
Lysander Wy *CNCK/NC* WS11 ....15 E3
Lytham *TAM/AM/WIL* B77................43 F4

M

Macadam Cl *BNTWD* WS7................28 D1
Mac Gregor Crs
  TAM/AM/WIL B77 ....42 C5
Macgregor Tithe *CRTAM* B79............4 C2
Madden Cl *RUGE* WS15....................9 F2
Madox Cl *CRTAM* B79....................40 D1
Magna Cl *GTWY* WS6 ....35 E1
Magnolia *TAM/AM/WIL* B77 ....42 D5
Magnus *TAM/AM/WIL* B77 ....50 B1
Maidstone Dr *BNTWD* WS7..............29 F3
Main Rd Brereton *RUGE* WS15 ....9 D2
Maitland *TAM/AM/WIL* B77 ....46 C2
Maldale *TAM/AM/WIL* B77..............47 F3
Malham Rd *TAM/AM/WIL* B77 ....47 F3
Mallard Cft *LICH* WS13 ....2 E2
Mallets Cnr *LICHS* * WS14..............32 C4
Mallicot Cl *LICH* WS13 ....3 G1
Malt House Rd *RUGE* WS15............18 D1

Malvern Dr *RUGE* WS15....................6 C3
Manifold Cl *BNTWD* WS7................29 F3
Manley Rd *LICH* WS13 ....3 H1
Manor Av *CNCK/NC* WS11..............14 D5
  GTWY WS6 ....25 C5
Manor Ri *BNTWD* WS7....................28 C4
  LICHS WS14..............3 F6
Manor Rd *POL/KGSB/FAZ* B78 ......44 C3
  TAM/AM/WIL B77 ....5 H4
Mansfield Cl *CRTAM* B79................40 D3
Mansion Dr *BNTWD* WS7................29 F5
Manston Vw *CRTAM* B79................41 H1
Manta Rd *TAM/AM/WIL* B77............50 A1
Maple Cl *BNTWD* WS7....................28 B2
Maple Crs *CNCK/NC* WS11..............24 C1
Maple Dr *HEDN* WS12....................10 D3
Maple Gv *LICHS* WS14....................3 K4
Maple Ri *TAM/AM/WIL* B77............42 D5
March Cl *GTWY* WS6......................34 D3
March Banks *RUGE* WS15................6 D4
Marconi Pl *HEDN* WS12..................12 A4
Margaret Dr *CNCK/NC* WS11 ....11 E5
Marigold Cl *HEDN* * WS12..............16 A3
Marina Crs *HEDN* WS12..................15 G1
Mariner *CRTAM* B79........................40 D2
Market Hall St *CNCK/NC* WS11 ......15 E5
Market Pl *CNCK/NC* WS11..............14 D5
Market Sq *RUGE* WS15....................7 E4
Market St *CRTAM* B79......................4 E4
  HEDN WS12..............11 H5
  LICH WS13..............2 C3
  RUGE WS15..............7 E4
Marlborough Ct *LICH* WS13 ....2 C5
Marlborough Wy
  TAM/AM/WIL B77..............46 A3
Marlin *TAM/AM/WIL* B77................50 A1
Marlow Rd *TAM/AM/WIL* B77 ....5 K2
Marmion St *CRTAM* B79....................5 F5
Marquis's Dr *RUGE* WS15................13 G1
Marrick *TAM/AM/WIL* B77..............47 F4
Marsett *TAM/AM/WIL* B77..............47 F4
Marshall St *TAM/AM/WIL* B77 ....5 K2
Marsh La *LICHS* WS14....................31 H4
  LICHS WS14..............33 E4
Marshwood Cl *CNCK/NC* WS11 ......15 G4
Marston Rd *BNTWD* WS7................11 F5
Martin Cft *LICH* WS13 ....21 C5
Martindale *CNCK/NC* WS11............15 G4
Marton Av *BNTWD* WS7..................28 C1
Mary St *HEDN* WS12......................11 H4
Maryvale Ct *LICHS* WS14................3 C5
Masefield Cl *BNTWD* WS7..............18 C5
  CRTAM B79..............4 C7
Masefield Dr *CRTAM* B79................41 F2
Masefield Gv *CNCK/NC* WS11 ....15 E2
Matlock Dr *CNCK/NC* WS11............15 G2
Mavis Rd *HEDN* WS12....................16 C2
Mavor Av *BNTWD* WS7 ....17 H5
Mawgan Dr *LICHS* WS14..................3 G6
Maxstoke Cl *TAM/AM/WIL* B77 ......49 H3
Maxtock Av *LICH* WS13 ....2 B7
Maxwell Cl *LICH* WS13 ....2 E4
Mayama Rd *POL/KGSB/FAZ* B78 ....45 E4
Maybank Cl *LICH* WS13 ....3 K3
May Cl *BNTWD* WS7......................18 B5
Maycroft Cl *HEDN* WS12................11 F4
Mayfield *TAM/AM/WIL* B77 ....47 F4
Mayfields Dr *BRWNH* WS8..............37 F2
Mayflower Dr *RUGE* WS15................6 C4
McGhie St *HEDN* WS12..................11 H5
McKie Wy *RUGE* WS15....................9 E2
Meadowbrook Rd *LICH* WS13 ....21 H3
The Meadows *RUGE* WS15................9 H2
Meadow Cft *HEDN* WS12................14 C1
  LICH WS13..............22 D5
Meadow Gv *GTWY* WS6..................29 F1
Meadow Hill Dr *CNCK/NC* WS11......15 G4
Meadow Lark Cl *HEDN* WS12..........15 H2
Meadow Pk *CRTAM* B79....................4 B3
Meadow St *TAM/AM/WIL* B77..........5 G6
Meadow Vw *BNTWD* WS7................29 F3
Meadow Wy *HEDN* WS12................16 A3
Meadway *TAM/AM/WIL* B77............16 A5
Meadway St *BNTWD* WS7................16 D4
Mease Av *HEDN* WS12....................29 F3
Medina *TAM/AM/WIL* B77................46 A3
Medway *TAM/AM/WIL* B77..............46 A3
Medway Rd *BRWNH* WS8................37 G2
Meerash La *BNTWD* WS7................39 E1
Meg La *BNTWD* WS7......................18 D5
Melbourne Crs *HEDN* WS12............16 D4
Melbourne Rd *HEDN* WS12............16 D4
Melbury Wy *CNCK/NC* WS11..........16 D2
Melford *CRTAM* B79........................40 C3
Melford Ri *HEDN* WS12 ....18 A5
Mellwaters *TAM/AM/WIL* B77 ....18 D1
Melmerby *TAM/AM/WIL* B77............47 F4
Melrose Dr *HEDN* WS12..................11 F4

Mendip Rd *HEDN* WS12..................11 G2
Mendip Wy *TAM/AM/WIL* B77........47 F3
Mercia Cl *CRTAM* B79....................40 D2
Mercian Wy *TAM/AM/WIL* B77........43 E4
Mercury Rd *CNCK/NC* WS11 ....15 G1
Mere Cft *CNCK/NC* WS11................26 D4
Merganser *TAM/AM/WIL* B77..........50 D1
Meriden Cl *CNCK/NC* WS11............24 B1
Merlin Cl *CNCK/NC* WS11................14 A4
  TAM/AM/WIL B77..............50 D1
Merrill Cl *GTWY* WS6......................35 E2
Mersey Cl *RUGE* WS15....................7 E2
Mesnes Gn *LICHS* WS14..................2 E5
Metcalf Cl *BNTWD* WS7..................29 E1
Metcalfe Cl *HEDN* WS12 ....12 A5
Mica Cl *TAM/AM/WIL* B77..............47 E2
Michigan Cl *CNCK/NC* WS11 ....15 H4
Mickleton *TAM/AM/WIL* B77............47 F4
Middle Entry *CRTAM* B79..................5 F4
Middlesmoor *TAM/AM/WIL* B77......47 F4
Middleton Rd *BRWNH* WS8..............38 C3
Middleway *HEDN* WS12..................16 D2
Midhurst Dr *HEDN* WS12................12 A4
Milburn *TAM/AM/WIL* B77..............47 F4
Mildenhall *CRTAM* B79....................41 H1
Millbrook Cl *HEDN* WS12................16 B5
Mill Crs *CNCK/NC* WS11..................15 H4
Millers V *HEDN* WS12......................16 B5
Millfield Rd *BRWNH* WS8................38 C5
Millicent Cl *HEDN* WS12..................15 H4
Millington St *RUGE* WS15..................7 E3
Mill La *BNTWD* WS7........................39 F1
  CNCK/NC WS11..............24 D4
  CRTAM B79..............5 G3
  POL/KGSB/FAZ B78..............45 F4
  RUGE WS15..............15 H3
Mill Pk *CNCK/NC* WS11..................15 G5
Mill Pool Rd *HEDN* WS12................11 H5
Mill Rd *BRWNH* WS8......................38 D5
Millside *RUGE* WS15........................8 B5
Mill St *CNCK/NC* WS11..................15 E5
Milner Dr *CRTAM* B79....................43 H2
Milo Crs *POL/KGSB/FAZ* B78..........45 F2
Milton Av *CRTAM* B79....................41 F2
Milton Rd *CNCK/NC* WS11..............15 E2
Minerva Cl *TAM/AM/WIL* B77 ....5 K2
Minister Pool Wk *LICH* WS13 ....2 D3
Minors HI *LICHS* WS14....................3 G7
Mitcham Cl *HEDN* WS12 ....11 H4
Mitchells Ct *CRTAM* B79....................4 E2
Mitre Rd *GTWY* WS6......................34 D2
Moat Dr *POL/KGSB/FAZ* B78..........48 D2
Moat La *GTWY* WS6........................35 G2
Monks Wy *TAM/AM/WIL* B77..........42 C4
Montley *TAM/AM/WIL* B77..............47 F4
Montrose Cl *CNCK/NC* WS11..........15 F1
Moon's La *GTWY* WS6....................34 D2
Moor Cl *BNTWD* WS7....................28 D2
Moore St *HEDN* WS12....................12 A4
Moorgate *CRTAM* B79......................4 D2
Moorland Cl *RUGE* WS15..................6 C3
Moorland Rd *CNCK/NC* WS11..........15 E1
Moor La *TAM/AM/WIL* B77..............5 J3
Moor St *BNTWD* WS7....................28 D2
Moreton St *CNCK/NC* WS11............15 F2
Morgan Rd *POL/KGSB/FAZ* B78......45 F2
Morley Rd *BNTWD* WS7..................28 D2
Morlings Dr *BNTWD* WS7................28 D1
Morpeth *TAM/AM/WIL* B77..............50 D1
Morston *TAM/AM/WIL* B77..............50 A3
Mossbank Av *BNTWD* WS7..............28 C3
Moss Cl *HEDN* WS12......................14 C1
Mossdale *TAM/AM/WIL* B77............47 F4
Moss Gn *RUGE* WS15......................6 C3
Moss Rd *CNCK/NC* WS11................15 G2
Moss St *CNCK/NC* WS11................15 G2
Mosswood St *CNCK/NC* WS11 ....14 C2
Mountain Pine Cl *HEDN* * WS12......11 G3
Mount Av *HEDN* WS12....................11 H4
Mountbatten Cl *BNTWD* WS7..........18 B5
Mount Cl *GTWY* WS6......................34 D2
Mount Pleasant *GTWY* WS6............35 E2
  TAM/AM/WIL B77..............45 H3
Mount Rd *BNTWD* WS7..................28 D2
  RUGE WS15..............8 B3
Mountside St *HEDN* WS12..............11 H4
Mount St *HEDN* WS12....................11 H4
Mowbray Cft *BNTWD* WS7..............18 A5
Mozart Cl *CNCK/NC* WS11..............16 A4
Muirfield *TAM/AM/WIL* B77............43 E4
Mulberry Rd *CNCK/NC* WS11 ....15 E3
Muldoon Cl *CNCK/NC* WS11............15 G2
Murton *TAM/AM/WIL* B77................47 F4
Myatt Av *BNTWD* WS7....................28 C2

N

Nailers Dr *BNTWD* WS7....................
Napier *TAM/AM/WIL* B77..................
Narrow La *BRWNH* WS8..................
Nash La *LICH* WS13..........................
Navigation Wy *CNCK/NC* WS11........
Neander *CRTAM* B79........................
Needwood HI *LICH* WS13 ....
Nelson Dr *HEDN* WS12....................
Nether Beacon *LICH* WS13..............
Netherbridge Av *LICHS* WS14..........
Nether La *BNTWD* WS7....................
Netherstowe *LICH* WS13..................
Netherstowe La *LICH* WS13..............
Neville St *TAM/AM/WIL* B77 ....
Nevill St *CRTAM* B79........................
Newbury Cl *GTWY* WS6....................
Newbury Rd *CNCK/NC* WS11 ....
Newcomen Cl *BNTWD* WS7..............
Newgate St *BNTWD* WS7..................
Newhall Crs *HEDN* WS12..................
Newhall Gdns *CNCK/NC* * WS11......
Newhall St *CNCK/NC* WS11..............
New Hayes Rd *HEDN* WS12..............
New Horse Rd *GTWY* WS6..............
Newlands Ct *HEDN* WS12................
Newlands La *CNCK/NC* WS11 ....
Newlyn Cl *LICHS* WS14....................
Newman Gv *RUGE* WS15..................
New Mill La *POL/KGSB/FAZ* B78......
New Penkridge Rd
  CNCK/NC WS11..............
Newport *TAM/AM/WIL* B77 ....
New Rd *BNTWD* WS7........................
  BRWNH WS8..............
  TAM/AM/WIL B77..............
New Rw *POL/KGSB/FAZ* * B78........
Newstead *CRTAM* B79......................
New St *BNTWD* WS7........................
  CNCK/NC WS11..............
  CNCK/NC WS11..............
  GTWY WS6..............
  HEDN WS12..............
  POL/KGSB/FAZ B78..............
  POL/KGSB/FAZ B78..............
  TAM/AM/WIL B77..............
Newton Rd *LICH* WS13 ....
Newtons College *LICH* * WS13..........
Nicholls Wy *HEDN* WS12..................
Nightingale Cl *TAM/AM/WIL* B77......
Nightingale Cl *HEDN* WS12..............
Nightingale Wk *BNTWD* WS7 ....
Nimbus *TAM/AM/WIL* B77 ....
Ninefoot La *TAM/AM/WIL* B77 ....
Ninian Wy *TAM/AM/WIL* B77 ....
Nirvana Cl *CNCK/NC* WS11..............
No Name Rd *BNTWD* WS7................
The Nook *GTWY* WS6......................
Norfolk Dr *POL/KGSB/FAZ* B78........
Norfolk Gv *GTWY* WS6....................
Norman Cl *CRTAM* B79....................
Northfields Wy *BRWNH* WS8 ....
North St *BNTWD* WS7......................
  CNCK/NC WS11..............
Northumberland Cl
  POL/KGSB/FAZ B78..............
Norton Cl *CRTAM* B79......................
Norton East Rd *CNCK/NC* WS11......
Norton Gra *CNCK/NC* WS11 ....
Norton Green La
  CNCK/NC WS11..............
Norton Hall La *CNCK/NC* WS11........
Norton La *BNTWD* WS7....................
  CNCK/NC WS11..............
  GTWY WS6..............
Norton Rd *HEDN* WS12....................
Norton Springs *CNCK/NC* WS11......
Norton Ter *CNCK/NC* WS11..............
Norwich Cl *LICH* WS13....................
Nursery Cft *LICH* WS13....................
Nursery La *POL/KGSB/FAZ* B78........
Nursery Rd *RUGE* WS15..................
Nuthurst Dr *CNCK/NC* WS11............
Nymet *TAM/AM/WIL* B77 ....

O

Oak Av *GTWY* WS6..........................
  HEDN WS12..............
Oakdene Rd *BNTWD* WS7................
Oakenfield *LICH* WS13......................
Oaken Gdns *BNTWD* WS7................
Oakenhayes Crs *BRWNH* WS8..........

es Dr *BRWNH* WS8 ....38 B3
 RUGE WS15 ....6 A3
 CNCK/NC WS11 ....15 F4
 LICHS WS14 ....3 F5
nds RUGE WS15 ....6 C4
 CI HEDN WS12 ....10 C5
 WD WS7 ....18 B5
 r RUGE WS15 ....9 H2
 ose RUGE WS15 ....6 B4
 Dr GTWY WS6 ....35 E2
 CK/NC WS11 ....14 A3
 I RUGE WS15 ....9 F2
 RUGE WS15 ....6 B4
 CNCK/NC WS11 ....24 C1
 BNTWD WS7 ....28 C5
 CRTAM B79 ....41 H1
 DN WS12 ....15 G1
 CRTAM B79 ....5 G2
 TAM B79 ....4 E2
 Rd BNTWD WS7 ....18 C4
 BRWNH WS8 ....38 C5
 CRTAM B79 ....4 E2
 Gv BRWNH WS8 ....38 B2
 el Rd RUGE WS15 ....7 E3
 Av CNCK/NC WS11 ....15 E3
 Rd CNCK/NC WS11 ....15 E3
 I GTWY * WS6 ....34 D1
 CNCK/NC WS11 ....25 H2
ng La
 /WIL B77 ....50 A2
sford Rd
 CNCK/NC WS11 ....15 G4
 CI
 B/FAZ B78 ....48 D2
 d HEDN WS12 ....17 E1
dge Rd
 CK WS11 ....14 C4
one La WNSFLD WV11 ..34 B4
 CNCK/NC WS11 ....25 F3
 rd BNTWD * WS7 ....28 A3
 WS7 ....28 D1
 v CNCK/NC WS11 ......14 C4
 GTWY WS6 ....35 E1
 3 ....21 F5
 15 ....7 E2
 /WIL B77 ....49 H2
 CRTAM B79 ....5 E3
 /WIL B77 ....5 G7
 ns BNTWD WS7 ....28 B1
 CK/NC WS11 ....25 F4
 TWY WS6 ....35 F3
 CNCK/NC WS11 ....15 F1
 TAM/AM/WIL B77 ......46 C5
 CI LICHS WS13 ....31 E3
 RTAM * B79 ....40 C2
 M/AM/WIL B77 ....50 D1
 HEDN WS12 ....16 A5
 CI HEDN WS12 ....16 C4
 M/AM/WIL B77 ....50 D2
 d BNTWD WS7 ....28 C4
 CI RUGE WS15 ....9 G2
 a BNTWD WS7 ....29 E5
ls Rd
 /WIL B77 ....7 E4
 RUGE WS15 ....7 E4
 Wy CRTAM B79 ....40 C3
 GTWY WS6 ....35 F3
 I CNCK/NC WS11 ....25 F1
 I CNCK/NC WS11 ....25 F1
 TWY WS6 ....35 F3

Park La *GTWY* WS6 ....35 F1
 LICH WS13 ....33 G1
 POL/KGSB/FAZ B78................44 D2
Park Rd BNTWD WS7 ....28 A1
 BNTWD WS7 ....28 D4
 CNCK/NC WS11 ....14 D5
 CNCK/NC WS11 ....27 E4
 TAM/AM/WIL B77 ....49 H2
Parkside TAM/AM/WIL B77 ......46 B3
Parkside La CNCK/NC WS11 ....14 A3
Park St CNCK/NC WS11 ....25 E3
 CRTAM B79 ....4 C3
 GTWY WS6 ....35 E1
Park View Ter RUGE WS15 ....6 D4
Parson St TAM/AM/WIL B77 ....46 B5
Partridge CI HEDN WS12 ....10 D4
Partridge Cft LICH WS13 ....2 E1
Passfield Av RUGE WS15 ....12 A4
Pasture Ga CNCK/NC WS11 .....14 C4
Patrick Ms LICH WS13 ....21 F5
Patterdale Rd CNCK/NC WS11 ..15 G3
Pavior's Rd BNTWD WS7 ....28 A5
Peace CI GTWY WS6 ....35 E1
Peakes Rd RUGE WS15 ....6 B4
Pear Tree CI CRTAM B79 ....43 H2
 HEDN WS12 ....10 C4
Pear Tree La BRWNH WS8 ....37 G2
Pebble CI TAM/AM/WIL B77 ......47 E1
Pebble Mill CI CNCK/NC WS11 ..15 F4
Pebble Mill Dr CNCK/NC WS11 ..15 F4
Peel CI POL/KGSB/FAZ B78 ......48 D2
Peel Dr HEDN WS12 ....11 C3
Peelers Wy TAM/AM/WIL B77 ...45 G3
Pelsall Rd BRWNH WS8 ....37 H5
Pendle HI HEDN WS12 ....16 A4
Pendrel CI GTWY WS6 ....35 E4
Penk Dr BNTWD WS7 ....29 F3
Penk Dr North RUGE WS15 ....6 B3
Penk Dr South RUGE WS15 ....6 B4
Pennine Dr CNCK/NC WS11 ......15 E4
Pennine Wy TAM/AM/WIL B77 ..47 E4
Penny Bank Ct RUGE WS15 ....7 E4
Penny Cress Gn CNCK/NC WS11 ..26 D5
Pennymoor Rd
 TAM/AM/WIL B77 ....47 E5
Pennys Cft LICH WS13 ....3 J1
Pentire Rd LICHS WS14 ....3 G6
Perrycrofts Crs CRTAM B79 ....41 H4
Peterborough Dr
 CNCK/NC WS11 ....16 A5
Peterhead TAM/AM/WIL B77 ....42 C4
Petersfield CNCK/NC WS11 ....15 F2
Peter's La BNTWD WS7 ....30 A4
Philip Gv CNCK/NC WS11 ....11 E5
Phoenix CI RUGE WS15 ....7 G4
Phoenix Rd CNCK/NC WS11 .....15 G4
Picasso CI CNCK/NC WS11 ....16 D1
Pillaton Dr HEDN WS12 ....10 C5
The Pines LICHS WS14 ....32 D2
Pine CI CRTAM B79 ....41 G1
 GTWY WS6 ....25 F5
Pine Gv BNTWD WS7 ....28 B4
Pine Tree CI HEDN WS12 ....11 E4
Pine Vw RUGE WS15 ....6 C2
Pinewood Av CNCK/NC WS11 ...14 D2
Pinewood CI BRWNH WS8 ....38 A2
Pinfold La CNCK/NC WS11 ....26 C5
 GTWY WS6 ....34 C2
Pinfold Rd LICH WS13 ....21 F5
The Pingle RUGE WS15 ....8 B1
Pingle La BNTWD WS7 ....29 F5
Pipers Cft LICH WS13 ....21 G4
Plantation La
 POL/KGSB/FAZ B78 ....40 A4
Plantation Rd HEDN WS12 ....11 D2
Plant La BNTWD WS7 ....27 H2
Plants CI GTWY WS6 ....35 G4
Platt St CNCK/NC WS11 ....15 C1
Ploughmans Wk LICH WS13 .....22 A3
Plovers Ri RUGE WS15 ....6 D4
Ponesfield Rd LICH WS13 ....21 H4
Ponesgreen LICH WS13 ....21 H4
Pool Av CNCK/NC WS11 ....27 F4
Poole Crs BRWNH WS8 ....37 H2
Poole's Wy BNTWD WS7 ....29 E2
Poolfield Rd LICH WS13 ....31 E3
Pool Meadow GTWY WS6 ....34 D3
Pool Meadow CI RUGE WS15 ......6 D5
Pool Rd BNTWD WS7 ....28 B5
 BRWNH WS8 ....38 B4
Pool Vw GTWY WS6 ....25 G5
Pope Gv HEDN WS12 ....11 F5
The Poplars CNCK/NC WS11 .....15 E2
Poplar Av BNTWD WS7 ....28 B3
 BRWNH WS8 ....38 C4
 CNCK/NC WS11 ....15 F2
Poplar Rd BRWNH WS8 ....38 C4
 GTWY WS6 ....35 F3

Poplar St *CNCK/NC* WS11 ....27 E3
Portland Av CRTAM B79 ....41 E1
Portland PI CNCK/NC WS11 ....24 C2
Portleys La POL/KGSB/FAZ B78 ...48 C3
Portobello RUGE WS15 ....7 E3
Post Office La RUGE WS15 ....8 B1
Pouk La LICHS WS14 ....39 G4
Power Station Rd RUGE WS15 ....7 F4
Price Av POL/KGSB/FAZ B78.......44 C3
Price St CNCK/NC WS11 ....15 E5
Primley Av TAM/AM/WIL B77 .....50 C2
Primrose Meadow
 CNCK/NC WS11 ....16 A4
Prince Rupert Ms LICH * WS13 ...21 F3
Prince Ruperts Wy LICH WS13 .....2 E1
Princess St BNTWD WS7 ....28 A1
 CNCK/NC WS11 ....15 E1
Prince St CNCK/NC WS11 ....11 E5
Priory Rd HEDN WS12 ....16 B2
 RUGE WS15 ....9 H3
Progress Dr CNCK/NC WS11 ....25 E2
Prospect Dr LICHS WS14 ....32 A3
Prospect Manor Ct HEDN WS12 ..16 A3
Prospect Rd BNTWD WS7 ....28 D3
Prospect St CRTAM B79 ....4 D2
Pullman CI TAM/AM/WIL B77 .....46 D2
Pump La RUGE WS15 ....6 C2
Purbrook TAM/AM/WIL B77 ....46 B4
Purcell Av LICH WS13 ....21 H4
Pye Green Rd CNCK/NC WS11 ....14 D4
 HEDN WS12 ....11 F3

Q

Quarry CI *GTWY* WS6 ....35 E1
 RUGE WS15 ....6 B5
Quarry Hills La LICHS WS14 ....32 B5
Queens Dr BNTWD WS7 ....28 B4
Queen St BNTWD WS7 ....28 B4
 CNCK/NC WS11 ....14 D5
 CNCK/NC WS11 ....15 E5
 GTWY WS6 ....34 D2
 LICH WS13 ....2 B4
 RUGE WS15 ....7 F5
Queensway CRTAM B79 ....41 F1
 RUGE WS15 ....9 F1
Quinton Av GTWY WS6 ....35 F1
Quonians La LICH WS13 ....2 D3

R

Radmore CI *BNTWD* WS7 ....27 H1
Radnor Ri HEDN WS12 ....15 H2
Railway La BNTWD WS7 ....18 A5
Railway St CNCK/NC WS11 ....25 E1
 CNCK/NC WS11 ....27 E4
Rainscar TAM/AM/WIL B77 ....47 E5
Rake HI BNTWD WS7 ....28 D1
Ramillies Crs GTWY WS6 ....35 F3
Ranger's Wk RUGE WS15 ....6 B4
Rangifer Rd POL/KGSB/FAZ B78 ...45 E4
Raven CI GTWY WS6 ....34 D2
 HEDN WS12 ....10 C4
 HEDN WS12 ....16 C2
Ravenhill CI RUGE WS15 ....9 F2
Ravenhill Ter RUGE WS15 ....9 F2
Ravenslea Rd RUGE WS15 ....9 F2
Ravenstone TAM/AM/WIL B77 ....47 E4
Rawnsley Rd HEDN WS12 ....12 C4
Raygill TAM/AM/WIL B77 ....47 E4
Rectory CI POL/KGSB/FAZ B78....48 D2
Redbrook CI HEDN WS12 ....16 B5
Redbrook La RUGE WS15 ....9 F2
Redcliff TAM/AM/WIL B77 ....42 C4
Redfern Dr BNTWD WS7 ....28 D4
Redhill CI CRTAM B79 ....41 F2
Redhill Rd CNCK/NC WS11 ....15 F2
Redlake TAM/AM/WIL B77 ....46 B4
Red Lion Av CNCK/NC WS11 ....27 E5
Red Lion Crs CNCK/NC WS11 .....27 E5
Red Lion La CNCK/NC WS11 ....27 E5
Redlock Fld LICHS WS14 ....31 G4
Redmond CI RUGE WS15 ....6 C3
Redmoor Rd RUGE WS15 ....18 B3
Redwell CI TAM/AM/WIL B77 ....5 K3
Redwing CI BNTWD WS7 ....29 F4
Redwing Dr HEDN WS12 ....10 C4
Redwood Dr BNTWD WS7 ....28 B1
 CNCK/NC WS11 ....15 F3
Reedmace TAM/AM/WIL B77 ....45 H2
Reeve La LICH WS13 ....2 C2
Regal CI TAM/AM/WIL B77 ....9 H4
Regency Ct RUGE WS15 ....9 F1

Reindeer Rd *POL/KGSB/FAZ* B78 ...44 D3
Relay Dr TAM/AM/WIL B77 ....47 F5
Rembrandt CI HEDN WS12 ....16 B4
Remington Dr CNCK/NC WS11 ...25 F1
Rene Rd TAM/AM/WIL B77 ....42 B4
Repington Rd North
 TAM/AM/WIL B77 ....42 D4
Repington Rd South
 TAM/AM/WIL B77 ....42 D4
Repton CI CNCK/NC WS11 ....24 B1
Reservoir Rd HEDN WS12 ....16 B2
Reynolds CI LICH WS13 ....21 H4
Ribblesdale Rd HEDN WS12 ......47 E5
Richmond CI CNCK/NC WS11 ...15 G1
 CRTAM B79 ....4 C3
Richmond Dr LICHS WS14 ....3 H5
The Riddings TAM/AM/WIL B77 ..42 B4
Rider's Wy RUGE WS15 ....6 B4
The Ridgeway BNTWD WS7 ....28 C4
Ridgewood Ri TAM/AM/WIL B77 ..42 D4
Ridings Brook Dr
 CNCK/NC WS11 ....15 G4
Ridings Pk CNCK/NC * WS11 .....15 G4
Rigby Dr CNCK/NC WS11 ....15 E2
Riley TAM/AM/WIL B77 ....46 B1
Ring Rd BNTWD WS7 ....27 H2
Ringway CNCK/NC WS11 ....15 E5
The Rise RUGE WS15 ....9 F2
Rishworth Av RUGE WS15 ....7 E3
Riverdrive POL/KGSB/FAZ B78.....4 E6
Riverfield Gv TAM/AM/WIL B77 ....5 J3
Riverside RUGE WS15 ....7 F3
Roach TAM/AM/WIL B77 ....50 A1
Robert CI CRTAM B79 ....41 E2
Robey's La POL/KGSB/FAZ B78 ..43 C4
 POL/KGSB/FAZ B78 ....47 C2
Robin CI HEDN WS12 ....10 C4
Robinia TAM/AM/WIL B77 ....42 D5
Robins CI GTWY WS6 ....34 D2
Robinson CI CRTAM B79 ....40 D2
Robinson Rd BNTWD * WS7 ......18 B5
Robins Rd BNTWD WS7 ....27 H3
Rochester Av BNTWD WS7 ....28 C1
Rochester Wy HEDN WS12 ....16 A5
The Roche BNTWD WS7 ....30 A1
Rocklands Crs LICHS WS13 ....3 C1
Rokholt Crs CNCK/NC WS11 .....14 C5
Roman CI BRWNH WS8 ....38 A2
Roman Ct TAM/AM/WIL B77 .....46 B5
Roman Vw CNCK/NC WS11 ....25 F4
Roman Wy CRTAM B79 ....40 D2
 LICHS WS14 ....3 H4
Romilly CI LICHS WS14 ....3 J4
Romney TAM/AM/WIL B77 ....46 C4
Rose Bay Meadow HEDN WS12 ..16 A4
Rosebery Rd TAM/AM/WIL B77 ..49 H3
Rosehill HEDN WS12 ....11 F3
Rose La BNTWD WS7 ....29 E2
Rosemary Av GTWY WS6 ....34 D1
Rosemary Dr HEDN WS12 ....14 D1
Rosemary Rd CNCK/NC WS11 ...24 D5
 TAM/AM/WIL B77 ....42 B5
Rose Wy RUGE WS15 ....6 C4
Rosewood CI TAM/AM/WIL B77 ...5 K5
Rosewood Ct TAM/AM/WIL B77 ...5 K5
Rosewood Pk GTWY WS6 ....34 D2
Rosy Cross CRTAM B79 ....5 F2
Rothay TAM/AM/WIL B77 ....46 C4
Rothbury Gn HEDN WS12 ....16 C4
Rotten Rw LICH WS13 ....2 E5
Roundhill Wy BRWNH WS8 ....38 C2
Rowan CI LICH WS13 ....3 H2
Rowan Gv BNTWD WS7 ....28 B3
Rowan Rd CNCK/NC WS11 ....14 C4
Rowley CI HEDN WS12 ....11 H3
 RUGE WS15 ....9 G2
Rufford CRTAM B79 ....40 D3
Rugeley Rd BNTWD WS7 ....19 E4
 BNTWD WS7 ....28 B1
 HEDN WS12 ....12 A5
 HEDN WS12 ....13 E4
 HEDN WS12 ....9 H2
Rumer Hill Rd CNCK/NC WS11 ..25 E2
Rush La TAM/AM/WIL B77 ....50 A4
Russett CI BNTWD WS7 ....28 C3
Rutherglen CI RUGE WS15 ....6 C4
Rutland Av RUGE WS15 ....8 D2
Rutland Dr POL/KGSB/FAZ B78 ..45 F3
Rutland Rd HEDN WS12 ....16 C5
Rydal TAM/AM/WIL B77 ....46 D5
Rydal LICH WS13 ....11 G3
Ryecroft Dr BNTWD WS7 ....28 C1
Ryknild St LICHS WS14 ....3 J7
Ryton TAM/AM/WIL B77 ....46 C4

S

Saddlers Cl *LICHS* WS14..............3 J3
Sadler Rd *BRWNH* WS8..............38 C4
Sadlers Ml *BRWNH* WS8............38 C5
St Aidan's Rd *CNCK/NC* WS11....15 H1
St Andrew Cl *HEDN* WS12..........17 E1
St Andrews *TAM/AM/WIL* B77......43 E5
St Anne's Cl *BNTWD* WS7..........28 A5
St Annes Rd *LICH* WS13.............21 H3
St Anthonys Cl *RUGE* WS15...........7 F5
St Augustine's Rd *RUGE* WS15......9 E2
St Austell Cl *CRTAM* B79..............4 D1
St Benedict's Rd *BNTWD* WS7......28 D3
St Bernards Cl *HEDN* WS12.........17 G2
St Catherines Rd *LICH* WS13.......21 H3
St Chad's Cl *CNCK/NC* WS11.......15 G2
St Chad's Rd *LICH* WS13..............2 D1
St Christopher Cl *HEDN* WS12.....17 E1
St Christopher's Dr
TAM/AM/WIL B77..................45 H3
St David Cl *HEDN* WS12............13 E5
St Editha's Cl *CRTAM* B79.............4 E3
St Edwards Gn *RUGE* WS15...........9 E1
St Francis Cl *HEDN* WS12...........17 E1
St George Dr *HEDN* WS12..........17 E1
St George's Wy
TAM/AM/WIL B77..................42 B5
St Giles Rd *BNTWD* WS7.............28 D3
St Helens Rd *LICH* WS13............21 H3
St Ives Cl *CRTAM* B79.................41 G3
St James Rd *CNCK/NC* WS11......14 C5
CNCK/NC WS11......................27 F4
St James Wk *BRWNH* WS8..........38 B5
St John's Cl *CNCK/NC* WS11.......24 D1
LICH WS13..............................2 C6
RUGE WS15...........................8 B1
St John's Ct *HEDN* WS12............16 C5
LICHS WS14............................2 D5
St John's Rd *CNCK/NC* WS11......24 D1
St John St *CRTAM* B79................41 G3
LICH WS13..............................2 C4
St Lawrence Dr *CNCK/NC* WS11...15 H4
St Luke's Cl *CNCK/NC* WS11.......24 C1
St Luke's Rd *BNTWD* WS7...........29 E3
St Margaret's Rd *CRTAM* B79......41 G2
LICH WS13.............................21 H3
St Mark's Cl *BNTWD* WS7...........29 E3
St Mary's Rd *LICH* WS13.............21 H3
St Mary's Wy *TAM/AM/WIL* B77...42 B5
St Matthew Cl *HEDN* WS12.........17 E1
St Matthew's Av *BNTWD* WS7......29 H2
St Matthew's Rd *BNTWD* WS7......29 H2
St Michael Rd *LICH* WS13.............3 F2
St Michaels Dr *HEDN* WS12.........17 E1
RUGE WS15............................9 G3
St Michael's Rd *RUGE* WS15........9 G3
St Patrick Cl *HEDN* WS12............17 E1
St Paul's Cl *LICHS* WS14.............15 H5
St Paul's Ct *TAM/AM/WIL * B77....49 H3
St Paul's Rd *BNTWD* WS7............29 E3
HEDN WS12...........................16 C3
RUGE WS15............................7 F5
St Peter's Cl *TAM/AM/WIL* B77....45 H3
St Peter's Rd *BNTWD* WS7..........29 E3
HEDN WS12...........................16 B2
St Stephens Ct *HEDN * WS12.......16 A2
St Stephen's Rd *BNTWD* WS7......28 D3
St Thomas Dr *HEDN* WS12..........17 E1
Salcombe Cl *CNCK/NC* WS11.......24 B1
Salisbury Cl *LICH* WS13..............22 A3
Salisbury Dr *CNCK/NC* WS11.......15 H5
Sallow Gv *BRWNH* WS8..............38 B3
Salop Dr *CNCK/NC* WS11............25 F1
Salter's La *CRTAM* B79.................4 E1
Salts La *POL/KGSB/FAZ* B78.......49 E3
Sam Barber Ct *HEDN * WS12........16 C4
Sambar Rd *POL/KGSB/FAZ* B78...45 E3
Samuel Cl *LICH* WS13.................22 A4
Sanderling Ri *BNTWD* WS7..........28 D1
Sandford St *LICH* WS13................2 C4
Sandown *TAM/AM/WIL* B77..........42 C4
Sandown Av *GTWY* WS6.............34 D1
Sandown Cl *BNTWD* WS7............18 B5
HEDN WS12...........................13 C5
Sandpiper *TAM/AM/WIL* B77........50 D2
Sandpiper Cl *HEDN* WS12...........12 A4
Sandringham Cl *BNTWD* WS7......18 A5
Sandy Gv *BRWNH* WS8..............38 B3
Sandy La *CNCK/NC* WS11...........14 A5
LICHS WS14..........................33 C5
RUGE WS15............................9 E1
Sandy Wy *TAM/AM/WIL* B77........46 D1
Sankey Crs *RUGE* WS15...............9 E1
Sankey Rd *CNCK/NC* WS11.........15 F3
Sapphire Dr *HEDN* WS12............16 A3

Sarah Challinor Cl *RUGE* WS15........7 E5
Saredon Rd *CNCK/NC* WS11........24 B5
GTWY WS6............................34 C1
Saturn Rd *CNCK/NC* WS11...........15 G1
Saunders Cl *HEDN* WS12............12 D5
Saxon Cl *GTWY* WS6..................35 G2
TAM/AM/WIL B77...................50 C1
Saxondrive *CRTAM* B79................5 C4
Saxon Mill La *CRTAM* B79..............5 C4
Saxon Wk *LICH* WS13.................31 E3
Scammerton *TAM/AM/WIL* B77....47 E5
Scampton Wy *CRTAM* B79...........41 H1
Scholars Ga *BNTWD* WS7............29 F3
School Av *BRWNH* WS8...............38 B4
School Cl *BNTWD* WS7................27 H1
CNCK/NC WS11.....................27 E3
School Crs *CNCK/NC* WS11..........27 E3
School La *BLOX/PEL* WS3............36 C2
BNTWD WS7.........................27 H1
POL/KGSB/FAZ B78................40 A2
RUGE WS15...........................18 C1
TAM/AM/WIL B77...................50 A2
School Rd *CNCK/NC* WS11...........27 E3
School St *TAM/AM/WIL* B77.........42 B5
School Wk *BNTWD* WS7...............27 H1
Scimitar Cl *CRTAM* B79................40 D2
Scotch Orch *LICH* WS13................3 H1
Scotia Rd *CNCK/NC* WS11...........14 D3
Scott Cl *LICHS* WS14..................2 D6
Scott Rd *TAM/AM/WIL* B77..........42 B5
Scott St *HEDN* WS12..................16 D3
Seabrooke Rd *RUGE* WS15............9 G3
Seafield *TAM/AM/WIL* B77............42 C4
Seaton *TAM/AM/WIL* B77.............46 C4
Seckham Rd *LICH* WS13................A2
Second Av *BRWNH* WS8..............38 C4
Sedgemoor Av *BNTWD* WS7.........28 D4
Seeds La *BRWNH* WS8................38 B4
Sefton Rd *TAM/AM/WIL* B77.........50 A3
Selker Dr *TAM/AM/WIL* B77..........42 B4
Setterfield Wy *RUGE* WS15............9 F2
Sevens Rd *HEDN* WS12...............17 C3
Severn Dr *BNTWD* WS7...............29 F3
Severn Rd *BRWNH* WS8..............37 G2
Seward Cl *LICHS* WS14.................3 G1
Seymour Cl *GTWY* WS6...............34 D3
Shaftesbury Dr *HEDN* WS12.........12 A4
Shaftsbury Rd *RUGE* WS15............9 E2
Shakespeare Av *LICHS* WS14........2 D7
Shakespeare Cl *CRTAM* B79.........41 F3
Shakespeare Gv *CNCK/NC* WS11...14 D2
Shakespeare Rd *BNTWD* WS7.......28 B1
Shanklin Cl *GTWY* WS6...............35 F1
Shannon *TAM/AM/WIL* B77..........46 C4
Shannon Dr *BRWNH* WS8............37 G2
Sharnbrook Dr *RUGE* WS15............6 C3
Sharon Wy *HEDN* WS12...............16 B3
Sharpe St *TAM/AM/WIL* B77.........42 D4
Shaw Dr *BNTWD* WS7.................18 C5
Shaw La *LICH* WS13....................2 B2
RUGE WS15...........................18 C2
Shaw's La *GTWY* WS6.................35 G1
Sheepcote La *TAM/AM/WIL* B77....46 C1
Sheep Fair *RUGE* WS15.................7 E4
Shelley Rd *BNTWD* WS7..............18 C5
CNCK/NC WS11.....................15 E1
CRTAM B79...........................41 E2
Shelton St *TAM/AM/WIL* B77.......46 C5
Shepherd Cl *LICH* WS13..............22 A4
Sheraton Cl *HEDN* WS12............11 F4
Sherbourne Av *HEDN* WS12.........16 C2
Sherbrooke Av
TAM/AM/WIL B77...................50 B1
Sherbrook Rd *CNCK/NC* WS11......14 C4
Sheriffs Cl *LICHS* WS14................3 K6
Sheringham Dr *RUGE* WS15............6 C3
Sherwood Dr *CNCK/NC* WS11......15 G3
Shetland Av *TAM/AM/WIL* B77......46 C5
Shirehall Pl *CNCK/NC* WS11.........15 H4
Shirelea Cl *BNTWD* WS7.............28 D1
Shoal Hill Cl *CNCK/NC* WS11........14 B5
Shooting Butts Rd *RUGE* WS15......6 A5
Shortbutts La *LICHS* WS14...........31 H4
Short La *GTWY* WS6...................35 E1
Short St *BRWNH* WS8.................38 B5
CNCK/NC WS11.....................15 F3
The Shrubbery *RUGE* WS15...........9 H2
Shugborough Rd *RUGE* WS15........6 C2
Shugborough Wy
CNCK/NC WS11.....................15 H5
Shuttington Br *CRTAM* B79..........43 G2
Shuttington Rd *CRTAM* B79..........43 E3
Siddons Cl *LICH* WS13................11 F4
Sidon Hill Wy *HEDN* WS12...........16 A3
Signal Wk *TAM/AM/WIL* B77.........46 D2
Silica Rd *TAM/AM/WIL* B77...........47 E2
Silver Birch Rd *CNCK/NC* WS11.....27 F5
HEDN WS12...........................10 D3

Silver Fir Cl *HEDN* WS12..............11 G3
Silver Link Rd *TAM/AM/WIL* B77....46 C3
Silver St *BRWNH* WS8.................38 A5
CRTAM B79...........................4 E3
Simcox St *HEDN* WS12...............16 B2
Simpson Rd *LICH* WS13...............21 H3
Siskin Cl *BNTWD* WS7................29 F4
Sister Dora Av *HEDN* WS12..........29 H2
Skidmore Av *TAM/AM/WIL* B77.....49 H3
Skipness *TAM/AM/WIL* B77..........42 B4
Skipton Pl *CNCK/NC* WS11..........24 B2
Skye Cl *TAM/AM/WIL* B77............46 C5
Skylark Cl *HEDN* WS12................10 C4
Slade Av *BNTWD* WS7................28 C1
Slade La *TAM/AM/WIL* B77...........49 H3
Slade View Ri *HEDN* WS12...........13 E5
Slang La *RUGE* WS15..................18 A1
Slingsby *TAM/AM/WIL* B77...........45 H5
Slitting Mill Rd *RUGE* WS15............8 B1
Smalley Cl *CNCK/NC* WS11..........15 G1
Smallridge *LICH* WS13.................21 F4
Smillie Pl *CNCK/NC* WS11............15 H3
Smithfield Ri *LICH* WS13................2 E2
Smith's Cl *BNTWD* WS7..............27 H2
Smithy La *LICH* WS13...................2 A1
TAM/AM/WIL B77...................46 C5
Snowdon Rd *CNCK/NC* WS11.......11 E5
Solway Cl *CRTAM* B79................41 F2
Somerset Av *RUGE* WS15..............8 D2
Somerset Cl *POL/KGSB/FAZ* B78..45 F3
Somerset Pl *CNCK/NC* WS11........15 E2
Sorrel *TAM/AM/WIL* B77..............42 D5
Southbourne Pl *CNCK/NC* WS11...14 D4
South Cl *CNCK/NC* WS11.............24 C1
Southern Cross *LICH* WS13............3 F4
Southfield Wy *GTWY* WS6............35 F2
Southgate *LICH* WS13.................24 B2
Southgate End *CNCK/NC* WS11....24 B2
Southwark Cl *LICH* WS13.............22 A3
Spade Gn *LICH * WS13.................30 A1
Spearhill *LICHS* WS14...................3 J4
Speechly Dr *RUGE* WS15...............6 D3
Speedy Cl *CNCK/NC* WS11...........15 E1
Spencer Dr *BNTWD* WS7.............28 A1
Spencer Rd *LICHS* WS14...............2 D7
Spenser Cl *CRTAM* B79.................4 C1
Spindlewood Cl *HEDN* WS12.........16 B5
Spinney Cl *BNTWD* WS7..............18 C5
CNCK/NC WS11.....................26 D4
Spinney Farm Rd
CNCK/NC WS11.....................24 B2
Spinney La *BNTWD* WS7.............18 B5
Spinning School La *CRTAM* B79.......5 F3
The Spires *LICHS* WS14.................3 J6
Splash La *HEDN* WS12................16 A3
Spode Pl *CNCK/NC* WS11............15 H4
Springfield Av *RUGE* WS15.............9 F1
Springfield Ri *HEDN* WS12............12 A5
Springfield Rd
TAM/AM/WIL B77...................46 A4
Springfields Rd *RUGE* WS15............6 D2
Springhill Rd *BNTWD* WS7............28 C3
BRWNH WS8.........................38 C5
Springhill Ter *RUGE* WS15..............9 F2
Springle Styche La *BNTWD* WS7...19 E5
Spring Meadow *GTWY* WS6..........34 D3
Spring Rd *LICH* WS13.................22 B4
Spring St *CNCK/NC* WS11............25 E1
Spruce Rd *HEDN* WS12................11 F2
Spruce Wk *RUGE* WS15................6 C1
Squires Ga *BNTWD* WS7.............29 E1
Squirrel Cl *HEDN* WS12...............10 C5
HEDN WS12...........................16 B4
Squirrels Hollow *BNTWD* WS7.......18 C5
Stafford Brook Rd *RUGE* WS15........6 A4
Stafford La *CNCK/NC* WS11.........15 H1
Stafford Rd *CNCK/NC* WS11.........14 D5
HEDN WS12...........................10 C4
LICH WS13............................21 E4
Staffordshire Wy *RUGE* WS15.........6 D1
Stafford St *HEDN* WS12...............16 C5
Stagborough Wy *HEDN* WS12........15 H2
Stag Cl *RUGE* WS15.....................6 B4
Stag Crs *CNCK/NC* WS11............27 E3
Stag Dr *HEDN* WS12..................10 C5
Staley Cft *HEDN* WS12................14 C2
Stamford Crs *BNTWD* WS7...........28 C1
Standedge *TAM/AM/WIL* B77.......46 D5
Stanley Rd *HEDN* WS12...............15 G1
Stapleford Gdns *BNTWD* WS7......29 F3
Station Ap *LICH * WS13................32 D1
Stationfields *CRTAM* B79................5 H2
Station Rd *BNTWD* WS7..............39 G1
GTWY WS6...........................25 F5
HEDN WS12...........................12 A5
LICH WS13............................2 D5
RUGE WS15...........................7 E4
Station St *GTWY* WS6.................35 E1

Steere Av *CRTAM* B79.......................
Stephenson Cl
TAM/AM/WIL B77.......................
Stevens Dr *HEDN* WS12...................
Stevenson Rd *CRTAM* B79................
Stevenson Wk *LICHS* WS14..............
Stile Cl *RUGE* WS15..........................
Stile Cop Rd *RUGE* WS15.................
Stirling Cl *CNCK/NC* WS11...............
Stockhay La *BNTWD* WS7................
Stoke's La *CNCK/NC* WS11..............
Stonehaven *TAM/AM/WIL* B77.........
Stonehouse Rd *RUGE* WS15.............
Stone Pine Cl *HEDN* WS12...............
Stonepit *TAM/AM/WIL* B77..............
Stoney Cft *CNCK/NC* WS11..............
Stoneyfields Cl *CNCK/NC* WS11......
Stoney Lea Rd *CNCK/NC* WS11.......
Stonydelph La
TAM/AM/WIL B77.......................
Stour *TAM/AM/WIL* B77....................
Stour Cl *BNTWD* WS7.......................
Stowecroft *LICH* WS13......................
Stowe Hill Gdns *LICH* WS13 ....
Stowe Rd *LICH* WS13........................
Stowe St *LICH* WS13.........................
Stratford Wy *CNCK/NC* WS11...........
Strathmore Pl *CNCK/NC* WS11.........
Strawberry La *GTWY* WS6................
Streets La *GTWY* WS6.......................
Stretton St *TAM/AM/WIL* B77..........
Stringers Hl *HEDN* WS12..................
Sturgeon's Hl *LICH* WS13.................
Stychbrook Gdns *LICH* WS13...........
Sudeley *TAM/AM/WIL* B77...............
Suffolk Wy *POL/KGSB/FAZ* B7 ......
Summerfield Cl
TAM/AM/WIL B77.......................
Summerfield Rd *BNTWD* WS7..........
TAM/AM/WIL B77.......................
Summer Gv *LICH* WS13....................
Summerhouse La *LICH* WS13...........
Summerside Av *HEDN* WS12 ....
Sunbeam *TAM/AM/WIL* B77..............
Sunbeam Dr *GTWY* WS6..................
Sunbury Av *LICHS* WS14..................
Sunfield Rd *CNCK/NC* WS11.............
Sunley Dr *HEDN* WS12......................
Sunningdale *TAM/AM/WIL* B77 ....
Sunrise Hl *HEDN* WS12.....................
Sunset Cl *CRTAM* B79.......................
GTWY WS6...............................
Surrey Cl *CNCK/NC* WS11................
RUGE WS15..............................
Surrey Dr *POL/KGSB/FAZ* B78.........
Sussex Av *HEDN* WS12.....................
Sutherland Rd *GTWY* WS6...............
Sutton Av *POL/KGSB/FAZ* B78.........
Sutton Cl *RUGE* WS15......................
Swallow Cl *RUGE* WS15...................
Swallow Cft *LICH* WS13....................
Swallowfield *CRTAM* B79..................
Swallowfields Dr *HEDN* WS12..........
Swan Cl *GTWY* WS6.........................
RUGE WS15..............................
Swanfields *BNTWD* WS7...................
Swan Ms *LICH* WS13.........................
Swanmote *CRTAM* B79......................
Swan Rd *LICH* WS13.........................
Sweetbriar Wy *HEDN* WS12 ....
Swift *TAM/AM/WIL* B77.....................
Swindale *TAM/AM/WIL* B77 ....
Swinfen Broun Rd *LICH* WS13..........
Swiss Lodge Dr
POL/KGSB/FAZ B78...................
Sycamore Cl *TAM/AM/WIL* B77 ....
Sycamore Crs *RUGE* WS15..............
Sycamore Gn *CNCK/NC* WS11........
Sycamore Hl *RUGE* WS15.................
Sycamore Rd *BNTWD* WS7...............
HEDN WS12...............................
Sycamore Wy *HEDN* WS12..............
Sykesmoor *TAM/AM/WIL* B77..........

T

Talbot *TAM/AM/WIL* B77....................
Talbot Rd *RUGE* WS15.......................
Talbot St *RUGE* WS15........................
Talland Av *TAM/AM/WIL* B77 ....
Tamar Cl *BRWNH* WS8.......................
Tamar Rd *TAM/AM/WIL* B77..............
Tame Av *BNTWD* WS7.......................
Tamedrive *POL/KGSB/FAZ* B78........
Tame Gv *CNCK/NC* WS11..................
Tame St *TAM/AM/WIL* B77.................

Cl *BRWNH* WS8 ....38 B2
Rd *LICHS* WS14 ....32 A4
B/FAZ B78.......................47 C3
/WIL B77 ....43 E3
/WIL B77 ....45 H3

Rd (Amington)
/WIL B77 ....42 B4

Rd (Dosthill)
/WIL B77 ....49 H1
St *LICH* WS13..................2 D3
M/AM/WIL B77 ....47 E5
 RUGE WS15.....................7 F4
/AM/WIL B77 ....5 H7
CH WS13 ....2 D2
CNCK/NC WS11................15 F2
Cl *CRTAM* B79 ....41 H2
 RUGE WS15.....................7 E4
 TWD WS7 ....29 F3
Ct *CNCK/NC* WS11........14 D3
Wy *HEDN* WS12.............10 C5
/AM/WIL B77.....................50 D3
 GTWY WS6.....................35 F1
 BNTWD WS7 ....28 D1
 HEDN WS12...................11 H4
 CRTAM B79 ....41 F2
CRTAM B79.........................4 D4
Av *GTWY* WS6................35 E1
v *BNTWD* WS7 ....18 C5
79 ....4 D1
CH WS13 ....21 F4
Dr *CRTAM* B79...............41 F2
RWNH WS8 ....38 C3
Cl *CNCK/NC* WS11........15 E5
UGE WS15 ....6 C3
vn Av *BNTWD* WS7.......28 C3
vn Dr *HEDN* WS12.........16 A5
ok *LICH* * WS13..............21 C5
TAM/AM/WIL B77 ....5 K5
 Rd *RUGE* WS15...............9 H3
CK/NC WS11.....................15 C1
CRTAM B79.........................40 D3
v TAM/AM/WIL B77 ....6 H4
UGE WS15 ....9 G2
Crs *BNTWD* WS7............28 C1
Cd *HEDN* WS12..............11 F4
Cft *GTWY* WS6................34 D3
 BNTWD WS7 ....27 H1
 BNTWD WS7 ....27 H1
M/AM/WIL B77..................42 B4
M/AM/WIL B77..................42 D4

een Rd
/WIL B77 ....50 C1
ICHS WS14.........................32 D1
La *RUGE* WS15...............19 E1
Rd *RUGE* WS15................7 E3
 TAM/AM/WIL B77 ....5 H6
POL/KGSB/FAZ B78 ....45 G4
M/AM/WIL B77..................49 H2

ey Park Homes
79 ....42 D3
M/AM/WIL B77..................42 B4
M/AM/WIL B77..................42 B5
Gv *HEDN* WS12..............16 A3
AM/AM/WIL B77................50 D2
M/AM/WIL B77..................47 E5
 HEDN WS12...................11 F2
w Rd *GTWY* WS6............35 F4
s *LICH* WS13.....................6 D4
E WS15 ....6 D4
Cl *HEDN* WS12...............16 C2
s *HEDN* WS12.................15 H4
NTWD WS7 ....28 C2
 TAM/AM/WIL B77 ....42 B5
M/AM/WIL B77..................42 D4
 LICHS WS14...................3 G6
Cl *LICHS* WS14.................3 C5
NTWD WS7 ....29 F3
Cl *CNCK/NC* WS11.........15 H5
NCK/NC WS11...................15 E1
ey Rd *LICH* WS13.............3 G3
Cl *RUGE* WS15..................9 F1
Cl *BNTWD* WS7...............29 G1
 GTWY WS6.....................35 E1
CNCK/NC WS11.................25 E1
Cl *HEDN* WS12................16 C2
POL/KGSB/FAZ B78 ....50 D5
 TWY WS6..........................35 F3
AM/AM/WIL B77................46 B1
M/AM/WIL B77..................46 B1
/AM/WIL B77 ....43 F5
 LICH WS13.....................21 H3
NTWD WS7 ....28 D4
36 ....35 E1
S14 ....32 D1
 TAM/AM/WIL B77.............42 C5
NTWD WS7 ....29 F3
S12 ....11 F3

Tudor Rw *LICH* * WS13 ....2 D4
Tudor Wy *GTWY* WS6.........34 D3
Tuke Pl *LICH* WS13..............21 F5
Tunnicliffe Dr *RUGE* WS15 ...6 D4
Turnberry *TAM/AM/WIL* B77 ...43 E4
Turner Cl *CNCK/NC* * WS11 ...16 B4
Tutbury *TAM/AM/WIL* B77.....45 H5
Tutbury Cl *HEDN* WS12........16 A3
Tutehill *TAM/AM/WIL* B77......47 E5
Two Oaks Av *BNTWD* WS7....27 H1
Tyne Cl *BRWNH* WS8.............37 G2

U

Ullswater *TAM/AM/WIL* B77....47 E5
Ullswater Pl *CNCK/NC* WS11...15 E5
Ulster Cl *LICHS* WS14............15 C3
Union Cl *TAM/AM/WIL* B77......5 H7
Union St *BNTWD* WS7............28 A1
  CNCK/NC WS11.................25 E3
Upfield Wy *RUGE* WS15...........6 C3
Uplands Cl *RUGE* WS15.........18 B1
Uplands Gn *RUGE* WS15...........8 D2
Upper Brook St *RUGE* WS15.....7 E5
Upper Cross Rd *RUGE* WS15.....9 E1
Upper Gungate *CRTAM* B79......5 F1
Upper Landywood La
  GTWY WS6.........................34 D3
Upper St John St *LICHS* WS14...2 D6
Upton Pl *RUGE* WS15..............9 E5
Uxbridge Ct *BNTWD* * WS7....28 B4
Uxbridge St *HEDN* WS12........16 A2

V

Vale Cl *LICH* WS13..................2 C1
The Valley *BNTWD* WS7........27 H1
Valley Gn *GTWY* WS6...........35 E2
Valley La *LICH* WS13...............3 H2
  TAM/AM/WIL B77...............46 B5
Valley Rd *HEDN* WS12...........12 B5
Valley Vw *BRWNH* WS8.........38 C5
Van Gogh Cl *CNCK/NC* WS11...16 B4
Vanguard *TAM/AM/WIL* B77....50 A1
Ventura Park Rd
  POL/KGSB/FAZ B78...........4 B6
Verdi Cl *LICH* WS13................22 A4
Vermont Gn *CNCK/NC* WS11...15 C3
Vernon Av *BRWNH* WS8........38 C5
Vicarage Cl *BRWNH* WS8.......38 C4
Vicarage Rd *BRWNH* WS8......38 B5
Vicars Cft *RUGE* WS15............7 F3
Victoria Dr *POL/KGSB/FAZ* B78...45 F4
Victoria Gdns *LICH* WS13.......31 F3
Victoria Rd *CRTAM* B79............5 C3
Victoria St *CNCK/NC* WS11....15 E2
  CNCK/NC WS11.................24 D1
  HEDN WS12.......................12 A5
Victory Av *BNTWD* WS7........28 B2
Victory Cl *HEDN* WS12...........16 C2
Viewfield Av *HEDN* WS12......11 F4
View St *HEDN* WS12..............11 F5
Vine La *CNCK/NC* WS11........24 D4
Viscount Rd *BNTWD* WS7......18 A5
Voyager Dr *CNCK/NC* WS11...25 F3
Vulcan Rd *LICH* WS13............22 C5

W

Wade St *LICH* WS13.................2 C4
Wainrigg *TAM/AM/WIL* B77....47 H5
Walhouse St *CNCK/NC* WS11...25 E1
Walkers Cft *LICH* WS13..........22 A4
Walkers Rd *HEDN* WS12.........12 B3
Walkmill La *CNCK/NC* WS11...24 D4
Walkmill Wy *CNCK/NC* WS11...24 D4
Wallace Cl *CNCK/NC* WS11....26 D4
Wallace Ct *GTWY* WS6...........34 D3
Wallace Rd *BRWNH* WS8........38 A4
Wall La *LICHS* WS14...............30 D5
Walnut Cl *CNCK/NC* WS11.....15 F3
Walnut Ct *RUGE* WS15.............9 G3
Walnut Dr *CNCK/NC* WS11.....15 F4
Walnut Gv *LICHS* WS14..........32 D2
Walsall Rd *CNCK/NC* WS11....25 E1
  CNCK/NC WS11.................26 D5
  GTWY WS6.........................35 G4
  LICH WS13...........................2 A5
  LICHS WS14.......................39 G4
Wardle Pl *HEDN* WS12...........14 D1
Wardles La *GTWY* WS6..........35 F3
Wardle St *CRTAM* B79..............4 C3

Ward St *HEDN* WS12..............11 F5
Warren Cl *HEDN* WS12...........17 E1
  LICHS WS14.........................3 K5
Warren Pl *BRWNH* WS8.........38 C5
Warren Rd *BNTWD* WS7.........28 C4
Warstone Rd *WOLVN* WV10...34 B3
Warwick Cl *CNCK/NC* WS11....11 E5
Warwick Rd *TAM/AM/WIL* B77...42 B5
Washbrook La *CNCK/NC* WS11...26 B5
Waterloo Bvd *HEDN* WS12.....16 C2
Watermint Cl *HEDN* WS12......16 C3
Waterside *RUGE* WS15.............9 F2
Waterside Ct *TAM/AM/WIL* B77...42 C4
Waterside Wy *BRWNH* WS8....37 G2
Watersmead Cl *HEDN* WS12...16 C2
Water St *BNTWD* WS7............28 A1
Watery La *LICH* WS13.............18 D3
  LICH WS13.........................22 A3
Watkiss Dr *RUGE* WS15............6 D4
Watling St *BRWNH* WS8.........38 D5
  POL/KGSB/FAZ B78...........51 H1
  TAM/AM/WIL B77...............45 H4
Watson Cl *RUGE* WS15.............6 D2
Wattfield Cl *RUGE* WS15...........9 G4
Wat Tyler Cl *RUGE* WS15.........6 D2
Waveney Gv *CNCK/NC* WS11...14 B5
Waverley Gdns *RUGE* WS15.....6 B3
Waverley Wk *LICHS* WS14......12 D6
Weaving Gdns *CNCK/NC* * WS11...15 F3
Wedgewood Cl *BNTWD* WS7...29 E2
Welford Rd *TAM/AM/WIL* B77...49 H2
Wellesbourne *CRTAM* B79......41 H1
Wellfield Cl *CNCK/NC* WS11....24 C5
Wellington Crs *LICH* WS13......23 F2
Wellington Dr *CNCK/NC* WS11...24 B1
  RUGE WS15.........................7 E5
Well La *GTWY* WS6.................35 G3
Wells Cl *CNCK/NC* WS11.......15 E1
Wembley La *BNTWD* WS7......27 G1
Wembury *TAM/AM/WIL* B77....42 B4
Wenlock *TAM/AM/WIL* B77......5 K6
Wentworth Cl *BNTWD* WS7....29 E2
Wentworth Dr *LICHS* WS14.....32 B4
Wesley Av *GTWY* WS6...........34 D1
Wesley Cl *BNTWD* WS7..........18 B5
Wesley Pl *HEDN* WS12...........12 A4
Wesley Wy *TAM/AM/WIL* B77...42 B5
Wessenden *TAM/AM/WIL* B77...47 E5
Wessex Cl *BRWNH* WS8.........38 B5
Wessex Dr *CNCK/NC* WS11....15 F4
Westbourne Av *CNCK/NC* WS11...14 D4
  GTWY WS6.........................25 E5
Westbourne Crs *BNTWD* WS7...28 D2
West Butts Rd *RUGE* WS15......6 B4
West Cannock Wy *HEDN* WS12...12 B2
West Coppice Rd *BRWNH* WS8...37 H4
West Dr *POL/KGSB/FAZ* B78...44 D2
Western By-Pass *LICH* WS13...21 E5
Western Rd *HEDN* WS12.........11 H5
Western Springs Rd *RUGE* WS15...6 D3
Westgate *HEDN* WS12............12 D5
West Hill Av *HEDN* WS12.......15 H1
Westminster Rd *CNCK/NC* WS11...11 E5
Westmorland Cl
  POL/KGSB/FAZ B78...........45 F3
Weston Cl *CNCK/NC* WS11.....16 B5
Weston Dr *GTWY* WS6...........35 E4
Weston Rd *LICH* WS13............21 G4
West St *CNCK/NC* WS11........25 E3
  CRTAM B79...........................5 C1
  TAM/AM/WIL B77.................5 G7
Westwoods Hollow
  BNTWD WS7.......................28 D1
Wetherall Cl *RUGE* WS15.........6 D1
Wharf Cl *LICHS* WS14...............6 D2
Wharf La *BNTWD* WS7............38 B1
Wharf Rd *RUGE* WS15..............9 E1
Wharwell La *GTWY* WS6.........35 H4
Whateley La *TAM/AM/WIL* B77...50 D3
Wheatcroft Cl *BNTWD* WS7....28 C4
Wheatlands Cl *HEDN* WS12....16 A5
Wheel La *LICH* WS13...............21 F5
Whinyates Ri *CNCK/NC* WS11...25 F1
Whitacre La *LICHS* WS14.........39 C5
Whitby Wy *CNCK/NC* WS11....24 C1
White Bark Cl *HEDN* WS12.....11 G3
White Horse Rd *BRWNH* WS8...38 A2
Whitehouse Crs *BNTWD* * WS7...28 D2
Whitesands Cl
  TAM/AM/WIL B77...............42 B4
Whitethorn Cl *HEDN* WS12....11 G3
Whitfield Rd *HEDN* WS12.......12 A4
Whitgreave La *RUGE* WS15......9 E2
Whiting *TAM/AM/WIL* B77......46 A5
Whitley Av *TAM/AM/WIL* B77...42 B4
Whittington Common Rd
  LICHS WS14.......................33 E5
Whitworth La *RUGE* WS15.......6 B3

Wigford Rd *TAM/AM/WIL* B77...49 H2
Wigginton Ldg *CRTAM* * B79...41 E2
Wigginton Rd *CRTAM* B79.......41 C3
Wightman Cl *LICHS* WS14.........3 J7
Wilcox Av *HEDN* WS12...........11 H4
Wilkin Rd *BRWNH* WS8...........37 G2
Wilkinson Cl *BNTWD* WS7......28 D1
Willett Av *BNTWD* WS7..........28 A4
William Morris Ct *RUGE* WS15...6 D2
William Morris Gv
  CNCK/NC WS11.................14 D2
Williamson Av *HEDN* WS12....17 G2
Willington Rd *CRTAM* B79......41 G2
Willoughby Rd *CRTAM* B79.....40 D2
The Willows *CNCK/NC* WS11...14 C5
  RUGE WS15.........................9 G3
Willow Av *BNTWD* WS7..........29 E3
Willowbank *POL/KGSB/FAZ* B78...45 G3
Willowherb Cl *CNCK/NC* WS11...16 A4
Willowsmere Dr *LICHS* WS14...32 D2
Willowtree Cl *LICH* WS13........21 H4
Wilnecote La *TAM/AM/WIL* B77...46 A2
Wilson Gv *CNCK/NC* WS11.....16 A4
Wiltell Rd *LICHS* WS14.............2 D6
Wimblebury Rd *HEDN* WS12...16 D5
Winchester Cl *LICH* WS13.......22 A3
Winchester Rd *CNCK/NC* WS11...15 G3
  POL/KGSB/FAZ B78...........4 A7
Windermere *TAM/AM/WIL* B77...47 E5
Windermere Pl *CNCK/NC* WS11...15 E5
The Windings *LICH* WS13..........2 B1
Windmill Bank *RUGE* WS15.....18 D1
Windmill Cl *CRTAM* B79..........41 F1
  LICH WS13.........................21 H4
Windmill La *LICH* WS13..........21 G4
  RUGE WS15.......................18 C2
Windrush Rd *CNCK/NC* WS11...11 E5
Windsor Cl *BNTWD* WS7.........18 A5
  CRTAM B79.......................41 H2
Windsor Rd *GTWY* WS6..........25 E5
Winsor Av *HEDN* WS12...........11 H5
Winstanley Rd *RUGE* WS15......6 D3
Winter Cl *LICH* * WS13...........22 B4
Wissage Ct *LICH* WS13.............3 G3
Wissage Cft *LICH* WS13............2 E1
Wissage La *LICH* WS13.............3 F1
Wissage Rd *LICH* WS13............3 F1
Witney Cl *CRTAM* B79............41 E2
Woburn *TAM/AM/WIL* B77........5 J7
Wolseley *TAM/AM/WIL* B77....46 C2
Wolseley Rd *RUGE* WS15..........6 D2
Wolsey Rd *LICH* WS13............21 F4
Wolverhampton Rd
  CNCK/NC WS11.................24 B4
  WOLVN WV10.....................34 B3
Woodcock Rd *RUGE* WS15.......6 C4
Woodcroft Av *CRTAM* B79........4 E1
Wood End La *LICH* WS13.........23 C4
Woodfield Cl *CNCK/NC* WS11...26 D2
Woodfield Dr *CNCK/NC* WS11...26 D2
Woodfields Dr *LICHS* WS14.......3 J7
Woodford Crs *BNTWD* WS7....28 D2
Woodford End *CNCK/NC* WS11...15 F2
Woodford Wy *HEDN* WS12......16 A5
Woodgreen *GTWY* WS6..........25 E4
Woodhaven *CNCK/NC* WS11...24 B3
Woodheyes Lawns *RUGE* WS15...6 C4
Woodhouse La
  TAM/AM/WIL B77...............42 D4
Woodhouses La *BNTWD* WS7...29 G3
Woodhouses Rd *BNTWD* WS7...30 A2
Woodhurst Cl *TAM/AM/WIL* B77...42 C4
Woodland Cl *HEDN* WS12.......11 H3
Woodland Ct *HEDN* WS12.......14 C2
Woodland Rd *TAM/AM/WIL* B77...42 D5
Woodland Wy *BNTWD* WS7....28 D3
The Woodlands *LICH* WS13.......3 C1
Wood La *HEDN* WS12..............16 A2
Woodman La *GTWY* WS6........25 E5
Woodpecker Wy *HEDN* WS12...16 A3
Wood Ridings *LICH* WS13........21 C5
Woods Cft *LICH* WS13...............2 B1
Woodside Pl *HEDN* WS12........14 D1
Woodstock Dr *HEDN* WS12.....10 C4
Woodthorne Cl *RUGE* WS15......6 C3
Wood Vw *RUGE* WS15..............9 F2
Woody Bank *GTWY* WS6.........35 E2
Wootton Cl *HEDN* WS12.........15 H3
Woottons Ct *CNCK/NC* WS11...15 F5
Worcester Cl *CNCK/NC* WS11...25 F1
  LICH WS13.........................21 H3
Wordsworth Av *CRTAM* B79.....4 C1
Wordsworth Cl *CNCK/NC* WS11...14 D2
  LICHS WS14.......................31 H4
Wordsworth Rd *BNTWD* WS7...28 C1
Wrekin Vw *HEDN* WS12..........10 C3
Wright's Av *CNCK/NC* WS11...15 F2
Wynyates *CRTAM* B79............40 D3

Wyrley Brook Pk
  CNCK/NC * WS11 ....**24** D3
Wyrley Cl *BRWNH* WS8 ....**38** B1
  LICHS WS14 ....**31** C1
Wyrley La *BLOX/PEL* WS3 ....**36** C3
Wyvern *TAM/AM/WIL* B77 ....**46** C1
Wyvern Gv *HEDN* WS12 ....**15** G1

Y

Yemscroft *GTWY* WS6 ....**35** G4
Yenton Cl *POL/KGSB/FAZ* B78 ....**45** F3
Yeovilton *CRTAM* B79 ....**41** H1

Yew Tree Av *LICHS* WS14 ....**3** J4
Yew Tree Cl *CNCK/NC* WS11 ....**27** E4
Yew Tree Rd *RUGE* WS15 ....**9** F2
York Cl *LICH* WS13 ....**22** A3
York Rd *CNCK/NC* WS11 ....**25** F2
Yorksand Rd
  POL/KGSB/FAZ B78 ....**45** E4

Z

Zion Cl *GTWY* WS6 ....

Index - featured places

Advance Business Park
  HEDN WS12 ....**15** H3
Aelfgar Sixth Form Centre
  RUGE WS15 ....**7** E4
Aldergate Medical Centre
  CRTAM B79 ....**4** E1
Amington Industrial Estate
  TAM/AM/WIL B77 ....**46** D1
  TAM/AM/WIL B77 ....**47** F2
Anglesey Business Park
  HEDN WS12 ....**16** C2
Ankermoor Primary School
  TAM/AM/WIL B77 ....**42** B4
Ankerside Shopping Centre
  CRTAM B79 ....**5** F4
Apex Business Park
  CNCK/NC WS11 ....**27** E4
Argyle Street Clinic
  TAM/AM/WIL B77 ....**42** B5
Arts Centre
  CRTAM B79 ....**5** F3
Ashcroft County Infants School
  CRTAM B79 ....**41** H2
Avon Business Park
  CNCK/NC WS11 ....**24** C2
Beauchamp Industrial Park
  TAM/AM/WIL B77 ....**46** A4
Beau Desert Golf Club
  HEDN WS12 ....**13** F3
Beechwood Business Park
  HEDN WS12 ....**15** H3
Beecroft Hill Special School
  CNCK/NC WS11 ....**14** D4
Belgrave High School
  TAM/AM/WIL B77 ....**46** C3
Belgrave Recreation Centre
  TAM/AM/WIL B77 ....**46** B3
Bennick Trading Estate
  CNCK/NC WS11 ....**25** F3
Birch Business Park
  CNCK/NC WS11 ....**25** F3
Birch Coppice Industrial Estate
  POL/KGSB/FAZ B78 ....**51** H2
Birds Bush County Primary School
  TAM/AM/WIL B77 ....**46** B4
Bishop's House
  LICH WS13 ....**2** C3
Blake High School
  HEDN WS12 ....**11** G5
Bonehill Industrial Estate
  POL/KGSB/FAZ B78 ....**45** E3
Boney Hay Primary School
  BNTWD WS7 ....**18** C5
Boston Industrial Estate
  RUGE WS15 ....**7** F3
Boswells Monument
  LICH WS13 ....**2** D3
Bridgeside Industrial Estate
  TAM/AM/WIL B77 ....**5** H7
Bridgeside Trading Estate
  TAM/AM/WIL B77 ....**45** H2
Bridgtown Business Centre
  CNCK/NC WS11 ....**25** E3
Bridgtown County Primary School
  CNCK/NC WS11 ....**25** E3
Brindley Business Park
  HEDN WS12 ....**15** H3
Brownhills Clinic
  BRWNH WS8 ....**38** B5
Brownhills Comprehensive School
  BRWNH WS8 ....**38** B3
Brownhills West JMI School
  BRWNH WS8 ....**37** G2
Burntwood Baths
  BNTWD WS7 ....**28** B3
Burntwood Health Centre
  BNTWD WS7 ....**29** E3
Burntwood Town
  Shopping Centre
  BNTWD WS7 ....**28** A2
Canal View Business Park
  RUGE WS15 ....**9** H2
Cannock Centre
  CNCK/NC WS11 ....**15** E5
Cannock Chase FC
  HEDN WS12 ....**11** H3

Cannock Chase High School
  CNCK/NC WS11 ....**15** E4
Cannock Chase Hospital
  CNCK/NC WS11 ....**15** E4
Cannock Chase Technical College
  CNCK/NC WS11 ....**14** D5
  CNCK/NC WS11 ....**25** E2
Cannock Industrial Centre
  CNCK/NC WS11 ....**24** D4
Cannock Park Golf Club
  CNCK/NC WS11 ....**14** D4
Cannock & Rugeley Cricket Club
  HEDN WS12 ....**17** E1
Cannock Sports Stadium
  CNCK/NC WS11 ....**15** F1
Cannock Wood Industrial Estate
  HEDN WS12 ....**13** G5
Cardinal Griffin RC School
  CNCK/NC WS11 ....**14** D3
Castle Museum
  CRTAM B79 ....**4** E4
Castle Pleasure Grounds
  TAM/AM/WIL B77 ....**5** F5
Cedars Business Centre
  CNCK/NC WS11 ....**24** C2
Chadsmead Primary School
  LICH WS13 ....**21** G5
Chadsmoor CE Junior School
  CNCK/NC WS11 ....**15** G2
Chadsmoor Infants School
  CNCK/NC WS11 ....**15** G2
Chancel Infant School
  RUGE WS15 ....**7** E3
Charnwood County
  Primary School
  LICH WS13 ....**22** A3
Chase Leisure Centre
  CNCK/NC WS11 ....**14** D4
Chase Park Industrial Estate
  BNTWD WS7 ....**27** H2
Chaseside Industrial Estate
  HEDN WS12 ....**15** H3
Chase Terrace High School
  BNTWD WS7 ....**28** B2
  BNTWD WS7 ....**28** C2
Chase Terrace Primary School
  BNTWD WS7 ....**28** B1
Chase Town CP School
  BNTWD WS7 ....**28** A4
Chase Town High School
  BNTWD WS7 ....**28** A5
Chasetown Industrial Estate
  BNTWD WS7 ....**28** A2
Chasewater Heaths
  Business Park
  BNTWD WS7 ....**18** B5
  BNTWD WS7 ....**27** G2
Chasewater Industrial Estate
  BNTWD WS7 ....**28** A3
Chasewater Light Railway
  CNCK/NC WS11 ....**37** G1
Chase Watersports Centre
  BRWNH WS8 ....**37** G1
Chasewood Park Business Centre
  HEDN WS12 ....**16** C5
Cheslyn Hay High School
  GTWY WS6 ....**34** B1
Cheslyn Hay Primary School
  GTWY WS6 ....**34** B1
Christ Church CE Primary School
  LICH WS13 ....**31** F2
Churchfield CE Junior School
  RUGE WS15 ....**7** E5
Conduit Road Industrial Estate
  CNCK/NC WS11 ....**27** E5
Coppice Side Industrial Estate
  BRWNH WS8 ....**37** H5
Coton Green Primary School
  CRTAM B79 ....**41** E2
Crossfield Industrial Estate
  LICH WS13 ....**3** K2
Delta Business Centre
  CNCK/NC WS11 ....**24** D3
Dosthill Primary School
  TAM/AM/WIL B77 ....**49** H2

Drayton Manor Family
  Theme Park
  POL/KGSB/FAZ B78 ....**45** E4
Drayton Park Golf Club
  POL/KGSB/FAZ B78 ....**45** E5
Driving Test Centre
  LICH WS13 ....**2** B4
East Cannock Industrial Estate
  HEDN WS12 ....**15** H3
Enterprise Industrial Park
  LICHS WS14 ....**32** D1
Erasmus Darwin Centre
  LICH WS13 ....**2** B3
Etching Hill CE Primary School
  RUGE WS15 ....**6** C3
Exchange Industrial Estate
  CNCK/NC WS11 ....**25** E3
Fairey Industrial Estate
  TAM/AM/WIL B77 ....**46** A4
Fair Oak School
  RUGE WS15 ....**6** C5
Fazeley Health Centre
  POL/KGSB/FAZ B78 ....**45** F4
First Community Health
  GTWY WS6 ....**35** F2
Five Ways Primary School
  HEDN WS12 ....**16** B4
Flax Hill Junior School
  CRTAM B79 ....**41** G2
Flaxley County Primary School
  RUGE WS15 ....**9** E2
Florendine Primary School
  TAM/AM/WIL B77 ....**42** C4
Frank Halfpenny Hall
  LICH WS13 ....**2** E3
Friary Grange Sports Centre
  LICH WS13 ....**21** F4
The Friary School
  LICH WS13 ....**21** E4
Fulfen Primary School
  BNTWD WS7 ....**29** F2
Gatehouse Trading Estate
  BRWNH WS8 ....**38** C3
Gentleshaw Primary School
  RUGE WS15 ....**18** C1
Glascote Comprehensive School
  TAM/AM/WIL B77 ....**46** C3
Glascote Heath Primary School
  TAM/AM/WIL B77 ....**46** C2
Glenthorne CP School
  GTWY WS6 ....**35** E1
Gorsemoor Primary School
  HEDN WS12 ....**16** B5
Great Wyrley High School
  GTWY WS6 ....**25** F5
Greenacres Primary School
  TAM/AM/WIL B77 ....**43** E4
Greenhill Health Centre
  LICH WS13 ....**2** E3
Green Industrial Estate
  HEDN WS12 ....**12** A4
Grove Park Industrial Estate
  CNCK/NC WS11 ....**25** E3
Hagley Park School
  RUGE WS15 ....**6** D5
Hammerwich Hospital
  BNTWD WS7 ....**28** D4
Hanburys Farm Community
  Primary School
  TAM/AM/WIL B77 ....**46** A3
Harrisons Institute & Sports Club
  GTWY WS6 ....**35** G3
Hawkes Green Medical Centre
  CNCK/NC WS11 ....**16** A4
Hawkins Colliery Sports Club
  GTWY WS6 ....**24** D5
Hawkins Sports Club
  GTWY WS6 ....**24** D5
Hazel Slade Primary School
  HEDN WS12 ....**13** E5
Heathfields Infant School
  TAM/AM/WIL B77 ....**50** C1
Heath Hayes Primary School
  HEDN WS12 ....**16** D4
Hedging Lane Industrial Estate
  TAM/AM/WIL B77 ....**50** A2

H Hayes Clinic
  HEDN WS12 ....
Highfields Primary School
  BNTWD WS7 ....
Hillsprings Clinic
  RUGE WS15 ....
Hobhill CE & Methodist
  Primary School
  RUGE WS15 ....
Hollies Business Park
  CNCK/NC WS11 ....
Holly Grove Primary School
  BNTWD WS7 ....
Huntington CP School
  HEDN WS12 ....
Jerome Primary School
  CNCK/NC WS11 ....
John Bamford Primary School
  RUGE WS15 ....
John Wood CE Infant School
  CNCK/NC WS11 ....
King Edward VI County School
  LICHS WS14 ....
King Edward VI Leisure Centre
  LICHS WS14 ....
Kingsmead High School
  HEDN WS12 ....
Kingston Court Shopping Arc
  CNCK/NC WS11 ....
Lakeside Industrial Park
  POL/KGSB/FAZ B78 ....
Lakeside Primary School
  TAM/AM/WIL B77 ....
Landywood County
  Primary School
  GTWY WS6 ....
Langton Medical Group
  LICH WS13 ....
Lark Hall Infants School
  CRTAM B79 ....
The Levels Industrial Estate
  RUGE WS15 ....
Lichfield Business Centre
  LICH WS13 ....
Lichfield Cathedral
  LICH WS13 ....
Lichfield Cathedral School
  (Bishop's Palace)
  LICH WS13 ....
Lichfield College
  LICH WS13 ....
Lichfield Cricket Club
  LICH WS13 ....
Lichfield Heritage Centre
  LICH WS13 ....
Lichfield Magistrates Court
  LICH WS13 ....
Lichfield Rd Industrial Estate
  CRTAM B79 ....
Lichfield Road Industrial Estate
  CRTAM B79 ....
  TAM/AM/WIL B77 ....
Lichfield RUFC
  LICHS WS14 ....
Lichfield Swimming
  Pools & Spas
  RUGE WS15 ....
Lichfield Trading Estate
  CRTAM B79 ....
Linkway Retail Park
  CNCK/NC WS11 ....
Littleton Business Park
  HEDN WS12 ....
Longford Industrial Estate
  CNCK/NC WS11 ....
Longford Primary School
  CNCK/NC WS11 ....
Longwood Primary School
  POL/KGSB/FAZ B78 ....
Manor CP School
  POL/KGSB/FAZ B78 ....
Maple Hayes Dyslexia School
  LICH WS13 ....
Marmion Junior School
  CRTAM B79 ....

e Trading Estate
  NC WS11 .... 15 G4
ntre
  B79 .... 5 F2
reen Industrial Estate
  VS14 .... 2 E5
Business Park
  SB/FAZ B78 .... 44 B2
P School
  J WS8 .... 38 C5
rimary School
  VS12 .... 11 G4
SB/FAZ B78 .... 45 F4
ndustrial Estate
  NC WS11 .... 15 G4
all Youth &
  unity Centre
  .... 2 C3
iness Estate
  VS12 .... 16 B3
Primary School
  VS6 .... 35 F1
Primary School
  B79 .... 4 E2
  B79 .... 4 E1
ounty Primary School
  NC WS11 .... 15 E1
rimary School
  NC WS11 .... 15 E2
ad Shopping Centre
  VS7 .... 28 D2
um of Cannock Chase
  VS12 .... 12 B5
owe County High School
  S13 .... 21 H5
nes Business Park
  NC WS11 .... 27 E5
nes Primary School
  NC WS11 .... 27 E3
nes School
  NC WS11 .... 27 E2
ields Primary School
  VS15 .... 9 G3
School
  M/WIL B77 .... 46 C2
ndustrial Estate
  VS12 .... 15 H3
Academy of
  e Dance
  WS7 .... 29 G4
  Infant School
  WS8 .... 38 B4
ports Centre
  NC WS11 .... 15 E5
tail Centre
  NC WS11 .... 25 F3
Primary School
  M/WIL B77 .... 45 H3
ol
  B79 .... 41 F2
County Primary School
  .... 9 E1
Medical Centre
  B79 .... 4 E3
ome Cinema
  NC WS11 .... 25 E1
Bowl
  SB/FAZ B78 .... 4 E5

Power Station Road
  Industrial Estate
  RUGE WS15 .... 7 F4
Prince of Wales Centre
  CNCK/NC WS11 .... 15 E5
Progress Business Centre
  CNCK/NC WS11 .... 25 E2
Prospect Business Park
  CNCK/NC WS11 .... 24 C2
Pye Green Valley CP School
  HEDN WS12 .... 11 G4
Queen Elizabeth Mercian
  High School
  CRTAM B79 .... 41 G3
Queens Croft School
  LICH WS13 .... 2 B5
Queen Street Industrial Estate
  BNTWD WS7 .... 28 B4
Quince Tree Special School
  TAM/AM/WIL B77 .... 42 D5
Ravenhill Primary School
  RUGE WS15 .... 9 F2
Redbrook Lane Industrial Estate
  RUGE WS15 .... 9 F3
Redhill Primary School
  CNCK/NC WS11 .... 15 E1
Red Rose Theatre
  RUGE WS15 .... 7 E4
Ridgeway Primary School
  BNTWD WS7 .... 28 C4
Ringway Industrial Estate
  LICH WS13 .... 22 A3
Riverside Industrial Estate
  POL/KGSB/FAZ B78 .... 45 G3
Rocklands Special School
  LICH WS13 .... 3 G2
Rugeley Health Centre
  RUGE WS15 .... 7 E5
Rugeley Tennis Club
  RUGE WS15 .... 6 C4
Rumer Hill Business Estate
  CNCK/NC WS11 .... 25 E2
Rydal Estate
  RUGE WS15 .... 7 F2
Ryecroft Shopping Centre
  BNTWD WS7 .... 28 B1
St Bernadettes RC JMI School
  BRWNH WS8 .... 38 B4
St Chads Stowe Primary School
  LICH WS13 .... 3 F2
St Elizabeths RC Primary School
  CRTAM B79 .... 41 F1
St Gabriels RC Primary School
  TAM/AM/WIL B77 .... 46 B3
St James Primary School
  BRWNH WS8 .... 38 B4
St Johns Preparatory School
  LICH WS13 .... 2 C5
St Joseph & St Theresa RC Primary
  School
  BNTWD WS7 .... 28 A3
St Josephs RC Primary School
  HEDN WS12 .... 16 A2
  LICHS WS14 .... 3 F5
  RUGE WS15 .... 9 E1
St Marys RC Primary School
  CNCK/NC WS11 .... 25 E1
St Michaels CE Primary School
  LICHS WS14 .... 3 F4

St Peter & St Paul RC
  Primary School
  LICH WS13 .... 21 H5
St Peters CE Primary School
  HEDN WS12 .... 16 B2
St Thomas More RC
  Primary School
  CNCK/NC WS11 .... 25 G5
Salters Meadow Health Centre
  BNTWD WS7 .... 28 B2
The Samuel Johnson
  Birthplace Museum
  .... 2 C4
Saxon Hill Special School
  LICHS WS14 .... 3 F6
Scotch Orchard County Primary
  School
  LICH WS13 .... 22 B5
Shires Industrial Estate
  LICHS WS14 .... 2 B7
Shopping Swan Corner Centre
  BNTWD WS7 .... 29 E3
Sir Robert Peel Hospital
  POL/KGSB/FAZ B78 .... 44 C2
Sofer Gallery
  CNCK/NC WS11 .... 25 E4
South Staffs Business Park
  CNCK/NC WS11 .... 24 C5
Springhill Medical Centre
  BNTWD WS7 .... 28 C2
Springhill Primary School
  BNTWD WS7 .... 28 D3
Springvale Primary School
  CNCK/NC WS11 .... 25 E1
Stafford College
  RUGE WS15 .... 7 F3
Staffs Moor Industrial Estate
  CRTAM B79 .... 4 C1
  CRTAM B79 .... 4 A2
Stoneydelph Infants School
  TAM/AM/WIL B77 .... 46 D3
Stoneydelph Primary School
  TAM/AM/WIL B77 .... 46 D3
Stowe CE School
  LICH WS13 .... 2 E1
Tame Valley Industrial Estate
  TAM/AM/WIL B77 .... 46 B5
  TAM/AM/WIL B77 .... 50 B2
Tame Valley Small
  Business Centre
  TAM/AM/WIL B77 .... 50 B1
Tamworth Assembly Rooms
  CRTAM B79 .... 4 E3
Tamworth Business Centre
  TAM/AM/WIL B77 .... 47 E1
Tamworth Business Park
  TAM/AM/WIL B77 .... 47 E1
Tamworth Castle
  CRTAM B79 .... 4 E4
Tamworth College
  CRTAM B79 .... 5 F1
Tamworth FC (The Lamb)
  TAM/AM/WIL B77 .... 5 G6
Tamworth Leisure Island
  (Snowdome Ski &
  Peaks Leisure Centre)
  TAM/AM/WIL B77 .... 5 F5
Tamworth Municipal Golf Club
  TAM/AM/WIL B77 .... 43 F5

Tamworth Sports Stadium
  TAM/AM/WIL B77 .... 46 C3
Thomas Barnes CP School
  POL/KGSB/FAZ B78 .... 40 A2
Three Spires Shopping Centre
  LICH WS13 .... 2 E4
Tolson Industrial Estate
  POL/KGSB/FAZ B78 .... 45 F4
Tolsons Mill Industrial Estate
  POL/KGSB/FAZ B78 .... 45 F4
Towers Business Park
  RUGE WS15 .... 9 H2
Trent Business Park
  RUGE WS15 .... 7 F3
Trent Valley Trading Estate
  LICH WS13 .... 22 A3
  RUGE WS15 .... 7 F2
Two Gates Primary School
  .... 45 H4
Two Gates Trading Estate
  TAM/AM/WIL B77 .... 46 A5
UCI Cinema
  CRTAM B79 .... 5 G4
Ventura Retail Park
  POL/KGSB/FAZ B78 .... 4 D6
Ventura Shopping Centre
  POL/KGSB/FAZ B78 .... 4 B7
Vicars Close
  LICH WS13 .... 2 B2
Walhouse CE Junior School
  CNCK/NC WS11 .... 14 C5
Walkmill Business Park
  CNCK/NC WS11 .... 24 C4
Watling Street Business Park
  BLOX/PEL WS3 .... 37 E2
Watling Street JMI School
  BRWNH WS8 .... 38 A3
West Chadsmoor Clinic
  CNCK/NC WS11 .... 11 E5
Western Springs Community School
  RUGE WS15 .... 6 D3
West Hill Primary School
  HEDN WS12 .... 11 H5
Whittington Grange
  Special School
  LICHS WS14 .... 33 H3
William Baxter Special School
  HEDN WS12 .... 11 G5
William Macgregor Primary School
  TAM/AM/WIL B77 .... 5 J5
Willows Primary School
  LICH WS13 .... 21 H4
Wilnecote Health Centre
  TAM/AM/WIL B77 .... 46 C5
Wilnecote Junior School
  TAM/AM/WIL B77 .... 46 C5
Wilnecote School
  TAM/AM/WIL B77 .... 50 C1
Wiltell Road Industrial Estate
  LICHS WS14 .... 2 D5
Woodlands Primary School
  TAM/AM/WIL B77 .... 42 B5
Wyley Brook Retail Park
  CNCK/NC WS11 .... 24 D3

Notes

Notes

Notes

AA Street by Street   QUESTIONNAIRE

Dear Atlas User
Your comments, opinions and recommendations are very important to us.
So please help us to improve our street atlases by taking a few minutes
to complete this simple questionnaire.

You do NOT need a stamp (unless posted outside the UK). If you do not want to remove this page from your street atlas, then photocopy it or write your answers on a plain sheet of paper.

Send to: The Editor, AA Street by Street, FREEPOST SCE 4598,
Basingstoke RG21 4GY

ABOUT THE ATLAS...

Which city/town/county did you buy?

Are there any features of the atlas or mapping that you find particularly useful?

Is there anything we could have done better?

Why did you choose an AA Street by Street atlas?

Did it meet your expectations?

Exceeded ☐   **Met all** ☐   **Met most** ☐   **Fell below** ☐

Please give your reasons

continued overleaf

ML

Where did you buy it?

For what purpose? (please tick all applicable)

To use in your own local area ☐   **To use on business or at work** ☐

Visiting a strange place ☐   **In the car** ☐   **On foot** ☐

Other (please state)

LOCAL KNOWLEDGE...

Local knowledge is invaluable. Whilst every attempt has been made to make the information contained in this atlas as accurate as possible, should you notice any inaccuracies, please detail them below (if necessary, use a blank piece of paper) or e-mail us at *streetbystreet@theAA.com*

ABOUT YOU...

Name (Mr/Mrs/Ms)

Address

Postcode

Daytime tel no

E-mail address

Which age group are you in?

Under 25 ☐   **25-34** ☐   **35-44** ☐   **45-54** ☐   **55-64** ☐   **65+** ☐

Are you an AA member? YES ☐   NO ☐

Do you have Internet access? YES ☐   NO ☐

Thank you for taking the time to complete this questionnaire. Please send it to us as soon as possible, and remember, you do not need a stamp (unless posted outside the UK).

ML